Islam Considered

Islam Considered

A CHRISTIAN VIEW

Margot Patterson

LITURGICAL PRESS
Collegeville, Minnesota

www.litpress.org

Cover design by Ann Blattner

All quotations from the Quran are taken from *The Koran*, A Phoenix Paperback, translated by J. M. Rodwell, with Foreword and Introduction by Alan Jones (London: Orion Publishing Group, 2001). Used by permission.

The Scripture quotations are from the *New Revised Standard Version Bible*, Catholic edition, © 1989 by the Division of Christian Education of the National Council of Churches of Christ in the U.S.A. Used with permission. All rights reserved.

1   2   3   4   5   6   7   8   9

Library of Congress Cataloging-in-Publication Data

Patterson, Margot.
    Islam considered : A Christian view / Margot Patterson.
       p.   cm.
    Includes bibliographical references.
    ISBN-13: 978-0-8146-1915-5
    ISBN-10: 0-8146-1915-0
      1. Islam.   2. Islam—Essence, genius, nature.   I. Title.

BP161.3.P37 2008
297—dc22
                                           2006019523

Contents

Preface

Shortly after the Sept. 11, 2001, attacks on the Pentagon and World Trade Center, I wrote a story on Islam for the *National Catholic Reporter*. More stories on Islam followed, and with it my interest in a religion that I and most Americans knew little about. I was already interested in the politics of the Middle East; studying the region's major faith tradition seemed a natural next step, particularly as the United States' enmeshment in the Middle East grew following the invasion of Iraq in 2003.

This book is an outgrowth of my reporting on Islam. It is a work of journalism, not of scholarship. There are many excellent scholarly books on Islam that will provide a far more complete, complex understanding of the religion. My goal in writing this book was to present a simple, readable account of the major tenets and practices of Islam and to provide readers some understanding of why the West in general and the United States in particular are regarded with antagonism by some Muslims. Necessarily, I have focused on politics as well as religion, if only because the hostility between the West and Muslims has its roots as much or more in contemporary geopolitics as it does in religious belief and practice.

Researching this book has exposed me to a religion, culture and history fascinating both in its own right and for the insights it has afforded me into my own religion and culture. I hope readers will find their own satisfaction in reading this brief introduction to Islam and that it leads them to further study of one of the world's great religions.

— Margot Patterson

CHAPTER 1

Faith and Practice

In a world of instant communications and rapid transportation, physical distances between nations are shrinking, yet the gulf between people of different backgrounds and faiths often seems larger than ever. Perhaps it's inevitable that friction arises as we come into close contact with people whose culture and customs are foreign to us. Often such clashes stem from an incomplete understanding of their history and our own and of the many values and aspirations we hold in common, notwithstanding differences in language, customs, beliefs, and experiences.

Since the attacks on the World Trade Center and the Pentagon on September 11, 2001, Americans have become increasingly conscious of and concerned about their relations with the Muslim world. Those relations have not only a political and an economic context but a religious one as well. While Americans cannot hope to understand one in isolation from the other, they may wish to begin their study of Islam with a look at its key beliefs and practices.

THE ORIGINS OF ISLAM

The story of Islam begins with Muhammad, the dynamic founder of a faith that now numbers over a billion adherents. But

1

Muhammad did not see himself as establishing a new religion. He believed that he was a religious reformer who was calling people back to the religion of Judaism and Christianity, but purged of the distortions these had acquired over the years. Muhammad saw his role as reviving the faith of Adam, Abraham, Moses, and Jesus. Ignorance had clouded the Arabs' vision, and it was Muhammad's role to convey to them God's will as it had been revealed to him. Muhammad saw himself as one in a line of prophets who brought a message to be heard and heeded. The message he preached was a relatively simple one of surrender (*islam*) to God's will, and the God he made known to his people was not a new and different God, but the God spoken of by the Jews and Christians. That is why when Christian Arabs pray, they use the same Arabic word for God—Allah—as Muslims do.

Like Jesus, the Muhammad of history can be difficult to disentangle from the Muhammad of faith. A rich corpus of traditions, both oral and written, developed around Muhammad in and after his lifetime. Called the *hadith*, these traditions constitute a significant source of information about Muhammad. The hadith include stories of what many Muslims believe Muhammad said as well as what he practiced (*sunna*) and form an abiding inspiration to Muslims of how they should live their life. Though Muslims see Muhammad as a man, not a God to be worshiped, he is regarded as an exemplar of excellence—a model to them of how a husband, father, ruler, teacher, and citizen should behave.

Muhammad has been vilified in some Western circles, and this is one of several reasons for the bitterness that has sometimes marked Christian-Muslim relations; but he was by all accounts an exceptional diplomat, warrior, statesman, and prophet. Historians and scholars who are not Muslims can agree that Muhammad must have been a remarkable man and an outstanding leader, one who was capable of uniting the warring tribes that lived in Arabia and of melding a new community based not on blood ties but on faith.

MUHAMMAD'S LIFE AND TIMES

Muhammad was born in what is now Saudi Arabia in the year 570 c.e. His father died before he was born, and his mother died when he was six, so Muhammad was raised by his grandfather and later his uncle. At the age of twenty Muhammad went to work for a successful businesswoman named Khadija. She was a widow, fifteen years older than Muhammad. Impressed by his talents and attributes, she asked him to marry her. Muhammad consented, and they were married when Muhammad was twenty-five years old. For another twenty-five years, until Khadija's death, the couple had what appears to have been a close and happy marriage. They had six children—two sons, who died in infancy, and four daughters, only one of whom outlived them.

Muhammad was a respected businessman in Mecca, so much so that he was called *al-Amin*, which means "the trusted one." Various accounts describe him as also devout, compassionate, astute, honest, and handsome. It is said that he loved solitude and would occasionally withdraw from society to a cave outside Mecca to meditate on the meaning of life and the problems of society.

At the age of forty Muhammad began experiencing dreams and visions. At first these visions troubled him, but after discussing them with Khadija and her cousin Waraqa ibn Nawfal, a Christian, Muhammad became emboldened to impart to a small group what had been revealed to him. He spoke of Allah, the God considered by the Arabs to be the most important god among the many divinities they worshiped at that time. Muhammad spoke of a Day of Judgment, when people would have to account for their actions. He urged people to be grateful to Allah for what they had and to express that gratitude by charity to others.

At the time of Muhammad, the Arabian Peninsula was populated by tribes. Some were engaged in farming, but most were nomadic. Desert and steppe dominated the one million square miles of Arabia. Bedouin tribes traveled from one area to another seeking water and pasture for their camels and sheep. There was no central authority, and fighting and factionalism were common. Social identity was organized around membership in an extended family. Several families comprised a clan; several clans constituted a tribe headed by a chief (*shaykh*).

Mecca, where Muhammad lived, was both a thriving commercial city and a place of pilgrimage. It was in Mecca that Arabs came to worship at the Kaaba, the sanctuary of 360 tribal idols built around a black, cube-shaped stone of meteoritic material. Most of the Arabs were polytheists, though a few of the Arab tribes had adopted Christianity. Jews also lived in the peninsula, as did Zoroastrians. Another native, pre-Islamic, monotheistic group called Hanifs traced their beliefs back to Abraham and yet were considered neither Christians nor Jews.

The world that gave rise to Muhammad and the emergence of a new faith was changing, the polytheistic ethos of Bedouin nomads giving way to a more commercial, urban society. The empires on either side of Arabia were Byzantium and the Persian Sasanid Empire; in both, a monotheistic faith had established itself as a state religion—Christianity in Byzantium and Zoroastrianism in the Sasanid Empire.

From the time Muhammad received his first revelation from God on the night Muslims call the "Night of Power and Excellence," when the archangel Gabriel appeared to him as he meditated in a cave on Mount Hira, Muhammad would receive ongoing revelations throughout his life. The thrust of these experiences was to highlight for him the perfect oneness of God. Idolatry was the ultimate sin, because it diminished God and divided the allegiance owed to God. The vocation of human beings was to serve God and to act as God's agents on earth.

Muhammad's message was initially not well received in Mecca. His emphasis on the one God, Allah, challenged the polytheistic ethos of his time as well as the interests of the powerful and privileged in Meccan society. Muhammad said that the rich had an obligation to the poor and the dispossessed, and he championed the rights of widows and orphans. He protested false contracts and usury and urged the imposition of a tax on wealth that would be distributed to the poor. His claim to prophetic leadership was an implicit challenge to the Quraysh clan, which administered the shrine in Mecca and collected revenues from it.

For ten years Muhammad struggled to convey his message. He won a small band of converts, including his son-in-law Ali ibn Abi Talib, who was to become a key figure in the history of Islam, and Abu Bakr, his future father-in-law, who would become Muhammad's successor as the first caliph, or leader, of the Muslim community. But for the most part, Muhammad and his followers in Mecca were ignored, abused, and on one occasion even attacked. On top of this disappointment, in 619 Muhammad's wife died and not long after his beloved uncle. In 620 Muhammad was invited by a delegation from the city of Yathrib, two hundred miles north of Mecca, to arbitrate a dispute between Arab tribes. Impressed by Muhammad's judgment and preaching, the visitors from Yathrib returned in 621 to seek counsel from him, and in 622 Muhammad and his followers were invited to settle in Yathrib, later known as Medina.

Muhammad's move to Medina in 622 with two hundred of his followers was a turning point in the life and ministry of the Prophet. This migration, called the *Hijra*, marked the first year of the Islamic calendar, which is calculated according to twelve lunar months. It bespeaks the communitarian nature of Islam that Muslims date their calendar not from the year Muhammad was born or died, but from the formation of the first Islamic community (*umma*) in Medina.

In Medina, Muhammad became the leader of a population comprised predominantly of nonnomadic farmers. Responding to the revelations that he continued to receive from God, he established his authority as the religious-political head of Medina. Most of the people in the city rallied to Muhammad, but some did not, including many of the Jewish population. These Jews, who came from Arab tribes that had converted to Judaism, had links to the Quraysh tribe in Mecca, which administered the sacred shrine and opposed Muhammad. Some of the Jews in Medina plotted to overthrow him.

For a decade the Muslims in Medina struggled against opposition. Eventually they triumphed. The Muslims banished or killed the recalcitrant Medinans who opposed Muhammad; they engaged the Meccans in battle and won; and they extended their influence to other areas of the Arabian Peninsula. By 631, distant tribes sent envoys to Medina to negotiate their submission to the authority of the new faith.

In 632, Muhammad died at the age of sixty-two after a pilgrimage to Mecca. Islam's rapid growth continued, however. The hundred years that followed saw the extension of Islam to many other parts of the Middle East. It spread north to Damascus, east to Persia, west to Egypt and the African continent. By 800, Muslims held land from what is now Switzerland to the eastern areas of India, an area larger than that which the Roman Empire at its peak had controlled. Today an Islamic empire no longer exists, but Islam continues to be a growing and dynamic faith. Like Christianity, Islam is a missionary religion whose adherents seek to share its message with non-Muslims.

KEY BELIEFS

Christians, certainly Catholic Christians, will recognize in Islam much that is familiar. Like Christians, Muslims believe in a Day of Judgment, when everyone will be held accountable for his or her deeds in life. Like Christians, they believe in the resurrection of the dead and eternal life. Muslims also believe in the existence of three realms, namely, heaven, earth, and hell.

While Muslims acknowledge sin, they do not subscribe to the concept of original sin held by Christians; rather, they believe that sin springs from human weakness and willfulness. It is not a state of being but a result of disobedience. The consequences of sin belong only to those who sin. Repentance is a matter of returning one's attention to God and making amends for misdeeds. The emphasis on the shame, guilt, and disgrace of sin sometimes found in Christianity is much less prevalent in Islam. Instead, Muslims focus much more on how inattention, carelessness, lethargy, and self-absorption distract men and women from their relationship with God. Remembrance is a key concept in Islam. One of the names the Quran uses to refer to itself is *al-Dhikr*, or "Remembrance," and Islam encourages an awareness of how forgetfulness of God creates an opening for an array of spiritual dangers.

Along with Christians and Jews, Muslims share a belief in revelation and prophecy. Like Christians and Jews, they have a scripture; with Christians and Jews it is the Bible, and for Muslims the Quran, or Koran. More will be said about the Quran later, but like the Bible, it is a record of prophecy and God's revelation to humankind. In addition, like Christians and Jews, Muslims trace their descent from Abraham. All three faiths are children of Abraham.

While Christians and Jews claim descent from Abraham through Isaac, Abraham's son with Sarah, Muslims trace their descent from Ishmael, Abraham's son with Hagar. Muslim tradition has it that Abraham, pressured by Sarah, who did not want her son, Isaac, to be outshone by his brother, took Hagar and Ishmael to or around Mecca, where he left them and where Ishmael became the ancestor of the Arabs of northern Arabia. When Abraham returned to Mecca, he and Ishmael built the Kaaba as the first shrine to the one true God. After Muhammad triumphed over the Meccans in battle, the first thing he did when he entered Mecca was to rededicate the shrine to Abraham and purge it of its tribal idols.

As this brief sketch demonstrates, Islam shares many of the tenets of Judaism and Christianity. Jews and Christians are recognized as "People of the Book," that is, people with a Scripture divinely inspired whose faiths merit respect. The word "Muslim" means one who submits to God. Muslims regard all the great monotheistic prophets in the Bible as Muslims.

The essence of Islam is contained in the short confession of faith called *shahada*, in which Muslims testify that "There is no god except the God, and Muhammad is his messenger," or "There is no God but Allah and Muhammad is his messenger."

The first part of this statement affirms the uniqueness of God, who is alone in power, mercy, and justice, the final cause of everything that happens in life. Muslims see God's oneness (*tawhid*) mirrored in the unity of the world, including the unity of the human family. Transcending divisions of race, nationality, and ethnicity, Islam teaches that all people are members of one single family; we are all related, and we share a common purpose and destiny. Its affirmation of God's unity finds a parallel in the all-embracing allegiance people owe to God. There can be no private corner of a person's life that does not include God. Thus religion cannot be separated from politics or economics. God has claim on the totality of our lives. The Quran states that the only unforgivable sin is *shirk*, that is, associating anything or anyone with God, thereby allowing a person, ideal, thing, or affection to usurp God's paramount role in a believer's life and distract from the love and loyalty owed to God.

The second half of the creed affirms Muhammad's role as messenger of God. In Islam, prophets are emissaries whom God has mercifully sent to inform men and women of their duties and to warn of the consequences of evil. Islam recognizes multiple prophets—Abraham, Noah, Moses, Jesus, among others—but Muhammad is the seal of the prophets, the final prophet whom God has sent. He is also a messenger from God. Messengers and prophets are not completely synonymous in Islam, for while all messengers are prophets, not all prophets are messengers. Messengers refer to prophets who have been entrusted with a sacred text for their community, as Moses, Jesus, and Muhammad were.

Through prophets, guidance has been provided to people on earth as to their duties to God and to their fellow human beings. Muslims believe that the prophets have lived in different places and times and delivered their message to particular peoples, but they do not differ from one another in their fundamental message. All the prophets call men and women to remember the divine oneness of God, whose very oneness is revealed in the multiplicity of peoples, prophets, and revelations. "And every people hath had its apostle," says the Quran (Sura 10:48).

Accordingly, the Quran encourages religious toleration. Recognizing the continuity of religious experience, Muslims should deal amicably with others who have been vouchsafed a revelation from God. "Dispute not, unless in a kindly sort, with the people of the Book; save with such of them as have dealt wrongfully with you: And say ye, 'We believe in what hath been sent down to us and hath been sent down to you. Our God and your God is one, and to him are we self-surrendered' (Muslims)" (Sura 29:45).

Like Christianity, Islam posits that upon a catastrophic event signaling the Day of Judgment, the dead will be raised and each person will be judged by God according to his or her actions in life, the standards of the community, and the particular message sent to their people by God. Muslim descriptions of the afterlife are more concrete and specific than those in Christianity. Eternity is depicted in both spiritual and physical terms as a fulfillment and fruition of life. The Quran speaks of beautiful gardens of flowing rivers, of a banquet at which guests will enjoy eternal peace, and, in a few verses, of enchanting companions called "the black-eyed ones" (*houris*). Western critics have translated the word "houris" as "virgins" and have spoken of them as a motive for suicide bombers today. Many Muslims would compare this with Christians believing they will receive a harp and wings when they go to heaven. Mainstream Muslims interpret the word "houris" allegorically; the houris are virgins insofar as they are purified souls. In any case, the delights of Paradise exist for all good Muslims, not just martyrs.

Hell is described equally graphically as an inferno. Sinners suffer in torment there for their sins, but the good may go directly to heaven. Some Muslims interpret the descriptions of heaven and hell literally; others see the descriptions in the Quran as metaphors of spiritual bliss and suffering.

Jesus plays a key role in Islamic eschatology. Like Christians, Muslims believe that there will be abrupt end times, at which point the Mahdi, that is, the prophesied redeemer of Islam, will arrive to rule the earth, followed by the Second Coming of Christ in Jerusalem, the destruction of the world, and the final judgment and resurrection of the dead. It is interesting to note that Jesus, not Muhammad, plays a key role in this final chapter of human history.

THE QURAN

The Quran is of inestimable importance in Islam, more important to Muslims than the Bible is to Christians, including even fundamentalist Christians. The Quran is God's revelation transmitted to Muhammad by the archangel Gabriel over a period of twenty-three years. Muslims consider it God's literal words. The word Quran means "recitation" and contains the messages recited or delivered by Muhammad and gathered together into a book, a task begun during Muhammad's lifetime and completed during the reign of the third caliph. Recitations of the Quran are an art and entertainment form in the Muslim world; they continue today and draw large crowds of people to listen to how the speakers choose to pronounce and intone the rhyming prose of the Quran, which is considered the finest work of classical Arabic.

Because the Quran is considered God's literal words, and Muhammad simply the recipient of them rather than their author or editor, both the form and content of the Quran are sacred. The message cannot be extracted from the words used to express it. The language itself is the vehicle of God's grace. Thus, while the Quran is often translated from Arabic into other languages so that non-Arabic-speaking people can read it, Muslims generally consider the translations necessary but not entirely satisfactory. They believe that one must learn Arabic to fully understand God's revelation in the Quran. The intrinsic role Arabic plays in God's final revelation is one reason why Quranic Arabic remains standard usage today, fourteen hundred years after the Quran was revealed to Muhammad.

Though Muslims believe that God chose to make his final revelation to the Arabic people, Islam acknowledges and honors previous revelations made to other peoples during history. The message of Islam is not unique or exclusive. The book of Moses, or the Torah, and the story of Jesus (*Injil*) are seen as being in agreement with the Quran. Moses and Jesus are regarded as among the greatest of God's prophets.

Christians may be particularly interested in the depiction of Jesus in the Quran. He is spoken of as Messiah, son of Mary, messenger, Word of God. The Quran shows him working miracles, though fewer than in the gospels, and portrays him as preaching an authentic message that it behooved his audience to follow. The virgin birth of Jesus is accepted, and Mary is a revered figure whose name appears more frequently in the Quran than in the New Testament. She is portrayed as a woman who completely accepted God's will, despite inevitable misunderstanding by members of her community and accusations of unchastity.

While the Quran presents Jesus as the second most important prophet after Muhammad, Muslims do not believe that Jesus was crucified or was the son of God. Given the power and grandeur of God, the idea that God would be born as a man in humble circumstances, suffer evil, and permit himself to be crucified seems absurd and impossible. God is without equal or offspring in their view, and they regard notions that Jesus was the son of God and was put to death as regrettable distortions of the truth. The absolute monotheism of Islam leads Muslims to reject the anthropomorphism found in Christianity. Talk of God as "father" or of humans being made in the image of God seems to them to blaspheme God's transcendent nature, which exceeds human beings' ability to understand and describe it.

In addition, Muslims do not understand why a God of power, justice, and mercy would demand the sacrifice of Jesus to atone for sin. Adam was forgiven for his sin, so why would more be demanded of his descendants? The idea contravenes their understanding of Islam as both God's final revelation and a return to the primordial monotheism that existed in the time of Adam and characterizes God's relationship to humankind. Muslims believe that Jesus was not crucified on the cross but escaped death and was taken up to heaven to be with God. The notion of the Trinity violates their understanding of God's oneness and seems to them a form of polytheism.

The Quran is organized into chapters called *suras*. The chapters do not depend on chronological order but are presented according to length; anyone can pick up the Quran at any point without missing prior information necessary to understand it. Some non-Muslims consider the Quran disorganized and confusing because of this and because the topic may shift from one paragraph to the next. Most Muslims consider the sequence of the suras holy because the Prophet was divinely inspired. The suras are composed of verses of unequal length, ranging from as little as 3 verses to 238. Many of the chapters recount or refer to events that take place in the Bible, but the Quran is not a straightforward book of history but a compendium of stories, exhortations, anecdotes, prayers, and descriptive and allegorical passages.

Every sura but one in the Quran begins "In the name of God, the Merciful, the Compassionate." Each sura ends with either the words Mecca or Medina to describe where the revelation was received. Usually shorter in length, the Meccan suras tell of the biblical prophets and deal with the fundamentals of faith, while the Medinan suras describe the early history of Islam and articulate how the community should be governed.

Not only do Muslims draw their main spiritual inspiration from the Quran, but the Quran has also been the source of studies of grammar, philology, literature, and law. Some scholars have compared the incarnation of Christianity with the "inlibration" of God in the Quran. God does not become embodied in the Quran as Christians think God becomes embodied in Jesus, but God's will and love and grace are made manifest in the book. The sense of this is so powerful that the word of God furnishes the inspiration for all Islamic art and civilization, whether this be calligraphy, chanting, Quranic recitation, carpets and textiles, or academic studies.

Modern biblical criticism as has been applied by scholars to the Bible is alien to most Muslims' view of their sacred Scripture. The Quran communicates a timeless message that speaks to men and women throughout history; their challenge is to implement God's message in their own era. Muslims acknowledge that the language of the Quran is a human language, but since human judgment did not create the Quran, they believe that human judgment cannot deconstruct it. The skeptical or neutral spirit that animated nineteenth-century biblical criticism and which was for that reason resisted by many churches (and continues to be rejected by some today) strikes Muslims as antithetical to the softening of the heart that the Quran should effect in readers or listeners.

THE FIVE PILLARS OF ISLAM

Islam is an action-oriented religion. Muslims are called to express their faith through the actions they perform in life. A good Muslim is not a passive or disengaged citizen, but one who actively contributes to the betterment of the community. While this can be done in any number of ways, being a good Muslim begins with practicing the essential obligations of the faith. These fivefold duties of Muslim practice are called the Five Pillars of Islam. They are:

1. declaration of faith
2. prayer
3. almsgiving
4. fasting during the month of Ramadan
5. pilgrimage to Mecca

Declaration of Faith

The declaration of faith, or *shahada*, has been described earlier. It is the statement "I witness there is no God but the God (Allah) and Muhammad is his messenger." Pious Muslims may repeat this confession twenty times a day or so. No other phrase is used as often. To become a Muslim, a person must only make this declaration, which confirms the two central tenets of Islam: God's transcendent power and Muhammad's role as his prophet and messenger.

According to scholars, faith (*iman*) consists of five elements: belief in one God, who alone is worthy of worship; belief in angels, who are messengers of God; belief in Scripture and prophets and their messages; belief in the Last Judgment; belief in divine

decree and predestination. The last is probably the most passion-
ately discussed element of Islamic faith. Just as Christians have
argued over the nature of providence versus free will, Muslims
have been divided over how much to attribute to God's will and
how much to the actions of men and women.

Angels play a role in Muslim cosmology very similar to their
role in Christianity. Islam regards angels as creatures of light who
serve God and act as intermediaries between him and his creation. Another supernatural creature, known as *jinn*, from which
the word "genie" derives, has the ability to interact with human
beings in ways both positive and negative.

The angels are said to record each person's good and bad deeds
in life. While God does not need the records to know people's
deeds, the recording of the angels encourages people to lead
good and God-fearing lives, confident in the knowledge that at
the Last Judgment they will receive justice from God. The angels
will stand with men and women when they account for their
actions to God. Those who have heeded God's commandments
will enjoy eternal life; those who have led unrighteous lives will
be thrown into the fiery pit of hell.

Prayer

One of the most commonly depicted images of Muslims is of
men in a mosque prostrating themselves to worship. This ritual
has a series of steps. Facing Mecca, the worshipers announce to
themselves the intention to perform *salat*, the name for the ritual
prayer. They begin by standing, then bend and touch their hands
to their knees. They rise and then drop to a kneeling position,
from which they touch their heads to the floor. They then rest
quietly on their heels. This process is repeated two, three, or four
times, depending on the time of day. During salat, worshipers
are enjoined to concentrate on prayer and not converse or look
around. Certain words are spoken at each of the positions, and
in addition to prayers for mercy and guidance, there is praise and
adoration. The first sura of the Quran, *Al-Fatiha*, or "The Opening," is always recited at each prayer period. This reads:

Praise be to God, the Lord of the worlds!
The compassionate, the merciful!
King on the day of reckoning
Thee only do we worship, and to Thee do we cry for help.
Guide Thou us on the straight path,
The path of those whom Thou has been gracious; —with
Whom Thou are not angry, and who do not go astray. (Sura 1)

Muslims are required to pray five times a day: before sunrise, at noon, mid-afternoon, sunset, and after nightfall. The hour of prayer is not up to the believer but is fixed. Because it depends on the rising and setting of the sun, the time changes with the seasons, and newspapers in Muslim countries usually print the exact time of prayer each day. It occurs in response to the call to prayer chanted by a *muezzin* from the tower, or minaret, of a mosque. This call to prayer is itself a prayer. The format is as follows:

1. "God is great" (repeated several times).
2. "I witness that there is no god but God" (said two times).
3. "I witness that Muhammad is the messenger of God" (said two times).
4. "Come to prayer" (said two times).
5. "Come to the good life" (said two times).
6. "Prayer is better than sleep" (this is said only at the dawn prayer).
7. "God is great" (said two times).
8. "There is no god but God."

Before they pray, Muslims are required to ceremonially cleanse their face and limbs. This is to purify themselves both physically and spiritually before seeking God in prayer. Bodily functions and contact with certain substances defile the believer. One washes one's ears to put away the thoughts that surround one and to pray in clear consciousness. The Prophet is quoted as saying, "Those who remember God when they perform their ablutions will have their whole body purified. But those who do not remember God at ablutions will not be purified except in those places where the water was applied" (Speight, *God Is One*, p. 33).

Worshipers face Mecca when they perform salat. They can pray individually or in groups. On Fridays worshipers visit the mosque to pray. This obligation has always been incumbent on men but not on women. Increasingly, however, women as well as men attend midday Friday prayer, particularly in the United States.

In addition to being places of prayer, mosques typically offer educational classes and serve as community centers. They are more informal than Christian churches, with people not only praying but relaxing, meditating, eating, and even sleeping inside the mosque. Furnishings are simple. Worshipers do not use chairs or pews but sit on the floor on mats, after removing their shoes before entering the mosque. A niche in the wall facing Mecca, called the *mihrab*, is the focal point for worship. This is unfurnished but often adorned with stuccowork or mosaic. There are no depictions of living creatures in the mosque so as to avoid idolatry, but floral and vegetal ornamental motifs are widely used.

Praying five times a day enables Muslims to develop *taqwa*, or reverence. Through taqwa, Muslims become aware of what draws them to God and what pulls them away from him. Taqwa is consciousness of God, alertness to God's will and awareness of the temptations that could keep believers from fulfilling it.

A Christian parallel to salat is the Liturgy of the Hours performed in Catholic and Anglican monasteries. One American who was raised Catholic and converted to Islam said he was drawn to Islam because it was monasticism for everyday life. Like Muslims, monks and contemplative nuns meet for prayer numerous times during the course of the day to give thanks and praise to God.

Prostrating oneself before God as Muslims do in salat seems foreign to many Christians, yet it is part of the Catholic tradition as well. Men preparing to be priests prostrate themselves during the sacrament of ordination. Priests also prostrate themselves before the altar on Good Friday, and members of some monastic orders prostrate themselves before the Blessed Sacrament instead of genuflecting. Salat is a form of embodied liturgical prayer expressive, some say, of both the outer and inner dimensions of Islam, for if the prayer is physical, even athletic, and communal, it is also internal and interior. The various postures represent the totality of human experience, from dependence to dignity.

The formal prayer of salat is a foundation of Islam but is not meant to exhaust Muslims' prayer life. Other prayers are often taken from or inspired by the hadith, the collection of Muhammad's sayings. Private, informal prayer is usually said in a worshiper's mother tongue rather than Arabic.

Unlike Christianity, Islam has no ordained leadership. The Friday prayers are led by a prayer master who delivers a sermon as well. Depending on the circumstances, the *imam* may also visit the sick, administer the mosque, instruct couples planning to marry, etc. Because they assume some of the same duties as priests and ministers, imams are sometimes compared to them, but there may be as many differences as there are similarities. In contrast to priests and ministers, imams are not required to be professionally trained or educated; laymen of faith considered to be of good character often serve as imams. As will be discussed later, Shi'i Muslims ascribe a special role and significance to the imam that Sunni Muslims do not.

Almsgiving

Islam is a religion that emphasizes social justice. Almsgiving, or *zakat*, is seen as an intrinsic element in bringing about a just society on earth. Faithful Muslims are required to donate 2½ percent of their total wealth each year to the needy or unfortunate. This is regarded more as an act of worship than a tax. In some Muslim countries the government collects the zakat. In others, offering zakat is left to the individual consciences of Muslims. In addition to helping prevent destitution and acting as a social welfare program, zakat is seen as having spiritual benefits. Those who give zakat are purified of selfishness and attachment to wealth and possessions, and those who receive zakat are helped to become free of envy and resentment.

The importance attached to zakat underscores the connection between faith and action in Islam. In the Quran, references to zakat are almost always preceded by a reference to prayer. While prayer is good, believers are also asked to demonstrate their faith through their commitment to others.

Since God is seen as the Creator of all things, including wealth, Muslims are expected to take seriously the duty of stewardship. They are trustees of God on earth, and they have a responsibility to use what they have been given for good.

Fasting

Like members of other religious traditions, Muslims practice fasting but confine it to the month of Ramadan, the ninth month of the Islamic lunar calendar. During Ramadan, Muslims abstain from food, drink, sexual activity, and other pleasures from before sunrise to sunset. It is a time when Muslims are encouraged to contemplate and practice the spiritual values of honesty, generosity, love, and devotion. The gulf between rich and poor diminishes as people of all classes are brought together to share a common experience of discipline and deprivation.

Ascetic self-denial of pleasure as a goal in and of itself is not promoted in Islam. Fasting is seen as a way of strengthening the will, growing in appreciation of God's gifts of food and drink, and heightening one's awareness of the hungry and unfortunate. During Ramadan one is meant to abstain not only from food and drink but from hurtful words or deeds. The Prophet said, "If you do not give up lying, there is no need for you to give up eating and drinking" (Speight, *God Is One*, p. 40). Hatred or envy is antithetical to the spirit of Ramadan and renders the fast invalid.

Muslims begin fasting during Ramadan from the age of thirteen. The ill, the elderly and infirm, pregnant women, travelers, soldiers in battle, and others in special circumstances are exempt from the fast but are expected to make it up at another point during the year.

The day after the end of Ramadan is the holiday of Eid al-Fitr, which translates as "The Feast of the Breaking of the Fast." The celebration extends for three days and is comparable to Christmas in its joyous spirit. People wear new clothes, exchange gifts, distribute food to the poor, and eat special delicacies to celebrate a time of hope, victory, and thanksgiving after the rigors of Ramadan.

Ramadan constitutes a decisive break with the normal pattern of life. There is a holiday feel during the month. For many Muslims, it is their favorite time of the year. Some say they never feel better. For others, Ramadan is a time of spiritual reflection and remembering, a purifying period in which believers try to rid their hearts of all that is not Allah and replace it with that which is "from Allah." Some will go to the mosque every evening to say the prayers that are said only during the month of Ramadan. Some may also recite the Quran from memory, one-thirtieth each night. Memorizing the Quran is considered an excellent achievement, one of the best ways of continuing the vitality of the living Scripture. Just as the Eucharist brings to Christian believers an experience of God's presence, the recitation of the Quran under proper circumstances can be an experience of divine presence for Muslims.

Ramadan commemorates two historical events: Muhammad's first revelation from God and the Battle of Badr in 624, when Muhammad and his followers triumphed over the Meccans despite being outnumbered.

Pilgrimage to Mecca

Making the pilgrimage (*hajj*) to Mecca is the last of the essential duties of Muslims. All Muslims are asked to make a trip to Mecca once in their lifetime if their finances permit. Pilgrims visit the compound of the Grand Mosque to worship at the Kaaba, which is revered as the first house of God built by Adam and then rebuilt by Abraham. Arabs have worshiped at the Kaaba for centuries, both before and after Muhammad rededicated it to Abraham. It is thought to replicate the throne of God, which is surrounded by angels.

Pilgrims walk around the Kaaba seven times, representing entrance into the divine presence. They walk—some run—seven times between two nearby hills, Safa and Marwa, in memory of Hagar, who, after she was repudiated by Abraham, is said to have run back and forth searching for water for herself and their son, Ishmael. Seeing her distress, the archangel Gabriel miraculously caused a spring to burst forth from the well. Pilgrims drink from the well, which is called Zamzam, and symbolically reject the devil's lures by throwing stones at a masonry pillar where Abraham rejected Satan's temptation in the Valley of Mina.

Sacred as the Kaaba is to Muslims, it is not meant to be worshiped as an idol. A hadith reports that Muhammad said that the destruction of the Kaaba is easier in the sight of God than the loss of an innocent life.

A key part of the hajj is visiting the Plain of Arafat, where Muhammad delivered his final sermon to the Muslim community before his death. From noon to sunset, pilgrims stand on the plain as Abraham stood before God. The pilgrimage ends with the sacrifice of an animal in memory of Abraham, who was willing to sacrifice his own son in obedience to God. Muslim tradition has it that this was Ishmael rather than Isaac.

The hajj reflects and reinforces in Muslims the strong sense of community that Islam instills. Coming from all points of the globe and all walks of life, Muslim worshipers are brought together in unity, a unity based on the oneness of God. Whatever their social or economic class, all on the hajj are equal before God. Pilgrims don white robes to circle the Kaaba and chant "Labbaika, Allahumma, labbaika" ("O God, here I am, at your service"). The white robes reflect the purification of the pilgrims, who must avoid sexual activity and improper speech and actions during the hajj.

The activities of the hajj connect Muslims to key events in their faith tradition (the construction of the first altar to God by Abraham, the first Muslim; the expulsion of Hagar and Ishmael; Abraham's sacrifice of his son in obedience to God; Muhammad's farewell speech to the Muslim community) and to key moments in the life to come. The white clothes that pilgrims wear symbolize their future passage from life to death. Wrapped in their burial shroud, those on the hajj forego all sorts of activities symbolic of life, from using perfume to carrying weapons, hurting animals (even an insect), or trimming their fingernails. All of the Five Pillars of Islam are compressed and expressed moment to moment in the hajj when pilgrims surrender their lives and will in service to God.

The pilgrimage occurs during the twelfth month of the year. In a spirit of communion with the pilgrims at Mecca, Muslims around the world sacrifice an animal on the same day as pilgrims do, on the tenth day of the hajj. Usually one animal per household is slaughtered for the Festival of Sacrifice, or Eid al-Adha, as it is called; ordinarily it is a sheep, but goats, cows, camels, and other herd animals are also acceptable. Some of the meat is eaten during the festivities that follow; most is given to the poor. As with Eid al-Fitr, the Feast of the Breaking of the Fast at the end of Ramadan, gifts are exchanged and special foods are prepared for the holiday.

The slaughter is not considered expiation for sin. Muslims do not believe that a blood sacrifice is necessary to eradicate the effects of sin. The festival should be seen in the context of pre-Islamic rituals in Arabia that regarded animal sacrifice as a way to purify the believer from sin. This belief was transformed in Islam into a commemorative rite meant to instill in worshipers a sense of honor and respect for parents and a willingness to sacrifice to God that which is most dear.

In addition to the hajj, there is a lesser pilgrimage called *umra*, which involves visiting Mecca at a time other than the designated twelfth month. Many pilgrims making the hajj go on to undertake a *ziyara* (visit) to Medina, where Muhammad is buried, but making the ziyara does not absolve believers from making the hajj.

====== CHAPTER 2 ======

Unity and Diversity in Islam

Islam, more than Christianity, is a practical faith. In this respect, it is more akin to Judaism, for while Christianity focuses on what people believe, Islam and Judaism focus on what people do. The importance that theology has for Christians, law has for Muslims. For both Muslims and Jews, disagreements within their faith have arisen primarily over interpretations of religious law rather than over matters of doctrine.

Regardless of their particular faith, all religious believers are necessarily faced with the question of what their religion means or demands of them. Muslims, Jews, and Christians alike ask themselves, What is God's will? What is God's law? For Muslims, this latter way of phrasing the issue is particularly apt to arise. Throughout Muslim history, law has been looked upon as a form of God's guidance, a blueprint for putting into effect the just society that God commands his followers to create. Religious law (*sharia*) is regarded as the expression of the divine will and is meant to encompass every imaginable aspect of human life. It continues to be a source of Muslim identity today, as is seen by the demand among some Muslims to reinstitute sharia.

If Westerners sometimes view the sharia as oppressive and harsh, many Muslims see it as providing a balance between individual and collective interests, a gift given by God to enable humankind to follow the straight path of Islam. Since Muslims think that faith is best expressed in action, they consider obedience to God's law their religious duty and the highest form of human behavior.

Islamic law classifies all human activities into five categories: obligatory; recommended; indifferent or permissible; reprehensible but not forbidden; forbidden. The ritual prayer of salat, for example, is obligatory, while giving to the poor is recommended but not obligatory. Divorce is reprehensible but not prohibited, whereas adultery, theft, and murder are absolutely forbidden. Breaking the law is considered a transgression against both society and God; it is both a crime and a sin.

Various schools of law developed within Islam, each with its own way of looking at religious law. By the thirteenth century, four schools predominated among Sunni Muslims, who constitute the great majority of Muslims. Named after their founders, these schools of law exercised influence in different parts of the Muslim world and continue to do so today. The Hanafi school is most prevalent in the Middle East and the Indian subcontinent; the Maliki in North, Central, and West Africa; the Shafii in East Africa and Southeast Asia; and the Hanbali school in Saudi Arabia.

Islamic law, or sharia, grew up alongside the dictates of local custom and laws instituted by various rulers. It developed over centuries after the time of Muhammad and draws on four sources: the Quran, the hadith, the consensus of the community, and analogy.

The Quran is the first and most authoritative source of Islamic law when it takes an unambiguous position on a certain matter. However, relatively little in the Quran deals with formal matters of law.

The hadith is the second source of Islamic law. Muhammad is regarded as the ideal Muslim, so his words and actions as they have come down to the Muslim community constitute a standard for how Muslims should behave. Here there is some difference among the schools of law. For instance, the Hanbali school in Saudi Arabia relies more on the prophetic tradition enshrined in the hadith as a source of law than the Hanafi school does.

Consensus is the third source of law, to be used if the first two sources do not offer a means of providing a legal ruling. The practice refers to a statement Muhammad is said to have made: "My community will not agree on an error." However, there is some controversy over who is to be consulted. According to the Shafii school, it refers to the entire community. Others have interpreted it to refer to the religious scholars alone, the *ulama*.

Analogy is the final means of reaching a legal decision and is used when the first three sources say nothing about the issue under consideration. By looking at what the law has decided in parallel situations, scholars arrive at a conclusion. Using analogy, legal scholars decided that because the Quran forbids the consumption of wine, other kinds of liquor should not be drunk either.

How do these principles translate into practice? One popular book on Islam gives as an example the question of whether electronic devices are permitted to call Muslims to prayer. For obvious reasons, neither the Quran nor the hadith has anything to say about the use of electronic equipment. But the Quran does encourage prayer, and one of the accepted traditions of the hadith tells of a Muslim named Bilal, who because of his strong voice was asked by the Prophet to call the people to prayer and sometimes stood on high ground the better to be heard. Using analogy, legal scholars might argue, as indeed they have, that microphones or electronic recordings do not change the prayer but only enable it to be better heard. Thus a microphone or an electronic recording of the call to prayer can be used. The specialist in Islamic law, or *mufti*, who gives his opinion on the matter issues a *fatwa*, or legal decision. If enough legal scholars concur with the fatwa, the ruling becomes part of Islamic law.

There is currently a debate taking place in some Muslim societies today about whether independent reasoning should be used in interpreting Islamic law. In the tenth century, Islamic law had developed sufficiently that Sunni Muslims declared that the gates of independent reasoning (*ijtihad*) had closed. It was held that jurists need only apply the laws that had already been instituted; they need not interpret them in light of the circumstances of the day. Many Muslims today argue against this and believe that independent reasoning is necessary for the revitalization of Islamic law. Shi'i Muslims, who have their own legal schools, have always held that independent reasoning should be used.

In most Muslim countries Islamic law exists alongside civil law and over the years has become restricted to family matters, governing marriage, divorce, and inheritance. In a few Muslim countries, such as Saudi Arabia and Iran, sharia is used to govern other matters as well. Many Westerners have heard of the severe punishments meted out to offenders in countries where sharia is applied to criminal matters. Capital punishment is prescribed for apostasy (forsaking Islam for another faith), murder, and adultery. Fornication, drinking alcohol, and sometimes adultery are punished by flogging. Those found guilty of theft may have their right hand cut off.

As in our own criminal justice system, sentences are perceived to be as much or more about deterring crime as about punishing offenders. High standards of evidence often mitigate the harshness of the punishments; for instance, adultery must be confirmed by four eyewitnesses to the act. It should be noted that the Quran exhorts Muslims to forgive repentant offenders and often gives judges considerable latitude in sentencing. Punishment is less harsh or sometimes is even waived if the guilty one confesses, if proof of guilt is lacking, or if the wronged party agrees to a monetary compensation. Cases where *hudud*, that is, Quranic punishment (amputation of the hands of thieves, stoning of adulteresses, flogging), are carried out are reserved for specific crimes that are seen as threatening the morality of the Muslim community.

While many liberal Muslims hold that the sharia must be interpreted in light of contemporary conditions and mores, others of a more conservative bent believe that if people are not observing the sharia, it is not the sharia that should be changed; rather, modern life should be changed to conform to the sharia. An analogous debate goes on today in Christian circles about if, when, and how biblical injunctions should be observed in legislating morality and setting policies both within the church and society at large.

Today the heart of the sharia in many Muslim countries has to do with the family, and it is here that its continuing influence is felt.

MARRIAGE AND FAMILY

In Islam, marriage is a sacred contract but not a sacrament. It is a contract entered into not just by two individuals but by two families. Islamic law stresses the free consent of both individuals entering the marriage as well as consultation with the parents of those marrying. The preferred marriage is between two Muslims, ideally within the extended family. Tradition has it that while a Muslim man may marry a Christian or a Jew, a Muslim woman should not marry outside her faith. This traditional prohibition is not always observed, however. Marriage is seen as the norm for people, providing children and mutual enrichment to both parties.

Divorce is discouraged but not prohibited. Tradition reports that Muhammad said, "Of all the permitted things, divorce is the most abominable with God." If a marriage is ended, the wife is usually assured financial independence. When a man and a woman marry, the man pays a dowry to the wife that becomes her personal property, and there is no expectation that she will spend it on maintaining the family. She is free to spend it, keep it, or lease it as she sees fit. It is legally easier for a man to divorce his wife than for a wife to divorce her husband, but the latter is permitted in cases of abuse, neglect, or abandonment.

Women receive only half of the inheritance of men; this is often justified on the grounds that women do not need to contribute their money to the upkeep of the household, whereas men are expected to take financial responsibility for the family.

Islam sees the roles of the sexes as complementary. A woman's role is primarily but not exclusively to tend to family and children; a man's role is to protect and provide financially for the family. The family holds a primary and central role and continues to be very strong in Muslim societies. Though polygyny is permitted, it is rare in most Muslim countries. The Quran enjoins that a man who has multiple wives treat them all justly, which is often interpreted as endorsing monogamy. "If ye fear that ye shall not be able to deal justly with the orphans, marry women of your choices, two, or three, or four; but if ye fear that ye shall not be able to deal justly (with them), then only one" (Sura 4:3).

Though many Muslim societies appear much more obviously patriarchal than in the West, where women's status has changed significantly during the last hundred years, the woman's position within the Muslim home is central. Islamic scholar Seyyed Hossein Nasr notes that if the man dominates social activity outside the home, "it is the wife who reigns completely in the home, where the husband is like a guest. . . . Women exert a much greater influence through the family within the whole of society than an outward study of what appears to be a patriarchal religious structure would indicate" (*Islam: Religion, History, and Civilization*, p. 102).

Since inclusive language has become an issue in some contemporary Christian churches, Christians may be interested to note that the Quran addresses both men and women separately as distinct sexes as well as together. Women are equal before the Divine Law and, like men, will be judged for their actions on earth. Muslim commentators point out that Islam raised women's status in the societies in which it first took root. It abolished female infanticide and gave women property and inheritance a thousand years before women won such rights in the Christian West.

Veiling, which is practiced in some Muslim societies but not all, is not intrinsic to Islam. In Muhammad's time most women did not wear veils. Veiling and seclusion (*purdah*) were customs assimilated from the Persian and Byzantine empires. Later, veiling became a common practice in the Middle East, especially for upper-class women. Christian and Jewish women in the region also wore veils and discontinued wearing them only in the nineteenth century, when, with the advent of colonialism, they adopted Western dress.

"Honor killings" have sometimes been mistakenly attributed to Islamic teaching. Such killings, in which a woman's sexual activity is considered to have dishonored her family and provoked her murder, are rooted in cultural practices that are not synonymous with Islam and extend beyond the Islamic world. Honor killings occur in many Middle Eastern societies, but not in Indonesia, the world's largest Muslim country. Honor killings have also taken place in Central and South America and in Europe, where Italy outlawed honor killing in 1981.

More will be said in the following chapter about women, but it should be noted that Islam originated in a patriarchal tribal society in which women had few rights, that much attributed to Islam is really due to the influence of local culture, and that there is a wide variance in how women are treated in Muslim societies. If Muslim women face legal and social discrimination in some countries, Muslim women have been elected heads of state in others (Pakistan, Bangladesh, Turkey, Indonesia). For these reasons, generalizations about the status of Muslim women need to be examined carefully.

ECONOMICS

While there is no stigma to accumulating wealth if it is acquired honorably, Islam stresses that wealth brings with it social responsibility. Muslims often speak of "the middle way" mentioned in the Quran, meaning that they try to balance individual and collective interests and steer clear of the excesses of both capitalism and communism. Muslims are encouraged to pursue spiritual advancement as well as the welfare of others by using their wealth to the benefit of the community. In this regard, Catholics will be reminded of the social teachings of their own church. Both religions warn of the danger of materialism and call believers to attend to the poverty and privations of others.

In addition to requiring zakat (almsgiving) as one of the essential duties for Muslims, Islam forbids usury. Collecting interest on loans, even on savings deposits, is seen as being contrary to Islam. Because the modern global banking system is built on interest-bearing loans, Muslims have sometimes been disadvantaged or handicapped by the prohibition of interest, but Islamic banking is increasingly common in Muslim countries today. In it, lenders as well as borrowers and depositors are asked to share the risk involved in borrowing money to finance a particular project.

The prohibition of interest derives from the view that money is a medium of exchange but has no value in itself, and that it is immoral to use money to make money. A similar view was held by the Catholic Church for many centuries. Because of it, Jews for centuries made their living by lending money to Christians. Jewish law forbade Jews to charge interest if they lent money to other Jews but allowed interest in transactions with Gentiles.

Islamic economics, like Islamic politics, derives from a view that God is the ultimate owner, ruler, and arbiter of all things. Neither politics nor economics can be detached from religion; to do so is typically seen as a betrayal of the central unifying message of Islam and its holistic vision of a society living in obedience to God. Partly for this reason, Westerners have sometimes charged Muslims with wanting to establish a theocracy. Muslims often note in response that there is no official clergy in Islam (thus "theocracy" is an inappropriate term) and that Islam can be compatible with a wide variety of political systems.

Christianity does not emphasize to the same extent as Islam the total demand that religious faith makes on believers. In the gospels, Jesus speaks of rendering unto Caesar what is Caesar's and unto God what is God's. But Christians who refer to this verse to underscore the differences between Christians and Muslims on church-state issues should remember that the separation of church and state in the West is not a Christian invention but owes its development to the effect of the Enlightenment. Christians, Catholics in particular, went through a long and painful period in which they struggled to reconcile their religious faith with the demands of the secular nation-state that developed in the last three hundred years. The idea of a united Christendom was once as persuasive to Christians as a transnational Islamic community or state is to some Muslims. Christians today continue to grapple with church-state issues, as is seen in the legislative and judicial debates about school voucher programs, monuments of the Ten Commandments in public places, abortion, pornography, and other issues. Since the establishment of Israel as a Jewish state in 1948, Jews have also struggled to define the place of religion in public life.

COMMUNITY

The replacement of tribal ties by ties to a community of faith was one of Muhammad's singular achievements. It was what enabled people of many different nationalities and languages to come together to form an Islamic *umma*, a word that can be translated as "people" or "nation" or "community." This solidarity in faith transcends national or ethnic identity. It is one reason why Islam has a reputation as an egalitarian religion with little history of racial prejudice.

This bond between Muslims is intended to take precedence over other tribal or ethnic ties and is often reflected in Muslims' concern about what is happening to their co-religionists in other parts of the world, whether this be Palestine, Afghanistan, Bosnia, Lebanon, or Iraq. While this has not prevented conflicts from erupting between Muslim societies from time to time any more than a common Christian faith has prevented Christian nations from making war on each other, Islam places a marked emphasis on sisterhood and brotherhood between Muslims.

Like Christianity, Islam is practiced in many different countries around the world—in Africa, the Middle East, South Asia, Europe, and the Americas. Not surprisingly, religious and cultural practices vary widely from place to place, just as they do in Christianity. While many Americans associate Islam with the Middle East, the five largest Muslim populations are in Indonesia, India, Pakistan, Bangladesh, and China, in that order. There are more Muslims who are African than Arab, and there are more Asian Muslims than there are African Muslims. Islam does not have denominations as Christianity does (Catholic, Methodist, Presbyterian, etc.), but divisions have developed over political succession, theology, Islamic law, and the meaning of history.

SHI'I AND SUNNI ISLAM

Islam, like Christianity, is not a monolithic religion. There are many schools and movements within it. The initial and by far the most important schism in Islam occurred over the issue of who should succeed Muhammad. When he died in 632, Muhammad had not designated a successor. How the Muslim community would react to his death, and whether the community would even survive it, must have been an open question. Abu Bakr, Muhammad's close companion and father-in-law and the man Muhammad had selected to lead the Friday prayers, announced Muhammad's death thusly: "Muslims! If any of you has worshiped Muhammad, let me tell you that Muhammad is dead. But if you worship God, then know that God is living and will never die" (Esposito, *What Everyone Needs to Know about Islam*, p. 45).

After some initial uncertainty, the elders of Medina chose Abu Bakr to be Muhammad's successor. He became the first *caliph*, meaning "representative" or "deputy." This decision to select the next leader of the Muslim community on the basis of who appeared most capable and qualified rather than on the principle of hereditary succession triggered the initial split between Sunni and Shi'i Muslims, with the Shi'a (the word means "party") believing that Muhammad's successor should be chosen from within Muhammad's family. The Shi'a (Party of Ali) believed that since Muhammad left no sons, the succession should pass through Muhammad's daughter Fatima and her husband Ali, who was Muhammad's cousin and closest male relative.

Ali, the son of Muhammad's uncle and Muhammad's adopted son, was the first male convert to Islam and was considered to have some of Muhammad's own remarkable qualities. The Shi'is were angry that Ali was passed over twice as caliph before being selected thirty-five years later as the third caliph, only to be assassinated a few years later. Ali and Fatima had two sons, one of whom was the charismatic Husayn, who was slain along with a band of followers in Karbala while on his way to claim the caliphate that he thought rightfully his. The martyrdom of Husayn and his followers constitutes one of the pivotal events in the Shi'i faith and is reenacted and commemorated each year.

The original division between those called Sunni (after *sunna*, the example set by Muhammad) and Shi'i was over the issue of Muhammad's successor, but over time the Shi'is, who constitute only about 15 percent of all Muslims, developed a somewhat different worldview from that of the Sunni. (It should be noted, however, that the divisions between Sunnis and Shi'is are much smaller than what they share; all Muslims practice the Five Pillars of Islam, revere the Quran, and respect the sharia.)

Unlike the Sunnis, who regarded the caliphs as protectors of the faith, with the right to lead the Friday prayers but without special religious inspiration or status, the Shi'is believe that eleven male descendants of Ali who followed him as *Imams* and acted as the political and religious leaders of the Shi'i community were virtually perfect, religiously inspired interpreters of God's message. While less than prophets, they commanded reverence and respect, and their word was authoritative. The Imams interpreted the inner spiritual meaning of the Prophet's words and actions and acted as spiritual guides to their people. In the Islamic seminaries developed by the Shi'a, the Imams' words constitute another source of law in addition to the four sources used by Sunni jurists.

Unwilling to recognize the authority of a Sunni caliphate, the Shi'i Imams generated suspicion among the caliphs, who watched them carefully and sometimes kept them in a state of virtual imprisonment. It is a Shi'i tenet of belief that the Imam was forced to go into hiding to protect himself and to ensure the continuation of his line. Shi'is hold that the hidden Imam will return at the end of the world as the divinely guided Mahdi (the expected one) to usher in a time of peace, prosperity, and justice for Muslims. In the interval the Shi'is are guided by *mujtahids*, experts qualified to exercise independent reasoning in the interpretation of Islamic law.

The Shi'is divide into several branches, the three most important being the Ithna Ashari, the Ismailis, and the Zaydis—or the Twelvers, the Seveners, and the Fivers—depending on their view of the legitimacy of those who followed Ali as Imam. The largest community of Shi'is are the Twelvers, or the Ithna Ashari, who recognized twelve Imams as successors to Muhammad. The twelfth disappeared without heirs in the ninth century after which he was said to have gone into hiding. The Twelvers dominate in today's Iraq, Iran, and Bahrain and are a significant presence in Lebanon, India, and Pakistan as well.

The Ismailis are sometimes called the Seveners because of their devotion to the seventh Imam, from whom they trace a line of Imams continuing down to the present. The Ismailis seized power in Tunisia in 909, and in 983 they wrested power from the Sunni caliph to establish their own rival caliphate in Egypt. The Fatimid dynasty (the name Fatimid emphasized the caliph's descent from Muhammad's daughter Fatima) lasted in Egypt from the tenth to the twelfth century. During this time, the Ismailis founded both the city of Cairo and the Al-Azhar University there, which ever since has been a major center of Muslim scholarship. Today the Ismailis are scattered among a number of different countries in South and Central Asia, Africa, and the Mideast, with the largest group, the Nizari Ismailis, led by the Agha Khan, forming prosperous communities in Europe and North America as well.

The Zaydis are much fewer in number than either the Ithna Asharis or the Ismailis. They founded a state in Yemen in 893, which lasted until 1963, and another in Tabaristan on the Caspian Sea. Political activists, the Zaydis broke with the other Shi'is in recognizing Zayd ash-Shahid rather than his half-brother as the fifth Imam. The Zaydis reject the notion of the Imam having divine power or special supernatural knowledge. They believe any descendent of Ali and Fatima is eligible to become Imam if he is intelligent, devout, and willing to fight for the position.

The figure of the Imam is central to the worldview of all the Shi'is. The concept of the hidden Imam is significant to Twelver Shi'ism not so much as literal fact but as representing the elusiveness of divine being in the world. Though Sunni Muslims also use the word "imam," they mean something very different from the Shi'i use of the word. For Sunnis, an imam is simply the person who leads the community in prayer. For Shi'is, the Imam is the guardian of religion who, even in hiding, serves human society and whose role in the faith is third only to those of God and Muhammad. In Iran, where Twelver Shi'ism is dominant, religious specialists and scholars known as *ayatollahs* represent the Imam in his absence. Devotion to the family or household of Ali is central to Shi'is, but some of the early Shi'i Imams were also revered by Sunnis, especially the great scholar and sixth Shi'i Imam, Ja'far al-Sadiq, for whom the major Shi'i school of law is named.

For most of their history, the Shi'is were an oppressed and disinherited minority whose worldview reflected their marginalized condition. Living under the domination of the Sunni majority, they came to value perseverance in suffering and the struggle of a righteous minority to resist injustice and restore God's rule on earth. In the twentieth century this emphasis on oppression and suffering became channeled into an active struggle to resist injustice. This reinterpretation particularly affected the Shi'is in Lebanon, who in the 1970s and 1980s struggled to gain greater political and economic rights and opportunities, and the Shi'is in Iran. The Shi'is have sometimes been portrayed in the West as a militant faction of Islam prone to violence, yet for most of their history they have eschewed political involvement and rejected worldly power. In the absence of the hidden Imam, the true leader of the umma, most Shi'is held that no government could be truly legitimate.

Sunnis are sometimes presented as the party of orthodoxy in Islam because of their greater number and their belief that the Muslim community is free to choose the best-qualified leaders it can. The Sunni position is that even a less-than-ideal leader is to be preferred to a civil war waged over his replacement. The designation of Sunnis as "orthodox" is somewhat misleading, however, as there is no central authority in Islam to define what is and what is not orthodox.

Differences between Sunnis and Shiʿis range from the initial disagreement over Muhammad's successor, to the role of saints, to where to place the hands in ritual prayer, to the institution of temporary marriage, which Shiʿis recognize but Sunnis do not, to the nature of God's attributes. The issue of religious authority continues to be the critical and overriding difference. In her book *Islam*, Karen Armstrong notes that Sunnis' trust in majority opinion and their more optimistic worldview has led them to emphasize that "God could be with the *ummah* even in times of failure and conflict. Regardless of flawed leaders, Muslims who abide by the sharia and lead holy lives can act as a counterweight to the corrupt conditions of their day and transform it into something corresponding to God's will" (p. 65).

Sunni Muslims pay particular respect to the first four caliphs who followed Muhammad and who are called the Four Rightly Guided Caliphs. They are seen as virtuous leaders who led the umma according to the dictates of the Quran and the sunna. The Umayyad dynasty followed, during which Muslims established an empire stretching from Spain to Central Asia. Sunni Muslims can and do look back on these and subsequent empires as a glorious period in their history confirming the validity of Islam's mission. But the dynamics and characteristics of empire are also different from the egalitarian society prescribed in the Quran, which set up a tension between faith and politics that is an enduring leitmotiv in Muslim history. An implicit separation of religion and politics took place during the course of these empires, and it was partly in protest against the splendor and arrogance of courtly culture that the sharia developed.

A third division within Islam took place when the Kharijites, a small extremist minority, broke with the mainstream Muslim community in the seventh century. Originally followers of Ali, the Kharijites later assassinated him because they saw his willingness to compromise with opponents as a sign of apostasy. Pious and puritanical, the Kharijites divided the world into two camps: Muslims and nonbelievers. Those Muslims who did not conform to their view of proper Muslim behavior were considered nonbelievers who could be excommunicated and even killed if they persisted in their nonrepentance. The Kharijites' rigorous, narrow standards and their willingness to use violence to overthrow a sinful and consequently illegitimate ruler have exercised an influence on several Muslim groups in history. The descendants of the Kharijites, now very few in number, are known as the Ibadi and live chiefly in Oman and on the island of Djerba near Tunisia.

SUFISM

The mystical tradition of Islam is called Sufism after the word *suf*, which means "wool," in reference to the rough woolen garments that ascetic Islamic mystics wore, much as Christian monks adopted a habit. Like mystics in other religions, Sufis stress the direct personal experience of God. Their goal is union with God through the extinction of self. Like Christian mystics and saints, the Sufis regard asceticism, self-sacrifice, and discipline as the means by which a person can curb greed, egotism, and laziness. This is the "greater jihad" sometimes referred to in Islam—the struggle to act in a manner that complies with sharia—as opposed to the "lesser jihad" to defend Islam. In pursuit of this goal, reading the Quran, studying the hadith, fasting, praying, denying material desires that could distract from God, fulfilling religious duties, and devoting one's self to fulfilling God's will are all means to *fana*, or extinction of self, and to the remembrance of Allah, of which the Quran often speaks.

Sufis have also regarded poetry, chant, and dance as means to this end. The Whirling Dervishes are a Sufi group famous around the world for their whirling dance, which transmits spiritual energies. The Sufi poet Rumi, who was the founder of the Mawlanah Order that the dervishes derive from and who died in 1273 in what is now Turkey, has achieved astonishing popularity in the West and is today one of the most widely read poets in the United States. The one-time slave and female mystic Rabiya al-Adawiya (d. 801) also exercised a great influence on Sufism. Rabiya's references to Allah as a lover and her fusion of the ascetic and the ecstatic call to mind such great mystics as St. Teresa of Avila and John of the Cross in the Christian tradition. The Sufi admonition "die before ye die," the emphasis on dying to self so that one can be reborn on a higher spiritual level, has obvious parallels with Christianity.

Sufism originally began as a reform movement within Islam. As Islam came to be associated with imperial power, there was a feeling that it had become corrupted by power and materialism. Some Muslims saw a corrective to this in rigidly emphasizing the laws and rituals of Islam. Sufis, on the other hand, rejected anything that smacked of legalism and believed that the corrective lay in following a spiritual inner path under the direction of a spiritual master or teacher.

By engaging in mystical exercises, Sufis hold that initiates can free themselves from petty concerns and purify their heart to the point where it accurately reflects the light of God. To this end, Sufis practice *dhikr*, which is meditation upon the names of God. The Quran mentions ninety-nine names of God that reveal his nature, and by chanting one as a mantra while controlling the breath, the Sufis found that they could achieve self-forgetfulness and, sometimes, ecstasy in their worship of God.

Through the ninth and tenth centuries, Sufism grew in Arabia, Egypt, Syria, and Iraq. It absorbed outside influences from Christian hermeticism, Buddhist monasticism, Hindu devotionalism, and neoplatonism. It became a mass movement in Muslim societies, influencing both Shi'i and Sunni Muslims.

The relationships between a Sufi master and his disciples eventually led to the formal establishment of organized Sufi brotherhoods or orders beginning in the twelfth century. Unlike Catholic orders, these were not under a central authority and usually did not require celibacy. Those who joined Sufi orders did not follow the route of Christian monastics in withdrawing from the world but under the tutelage of a Sufi master pursued an interior path while living in society. Sufi brotherhoods were frequently the great missionaries of Islam; their willingness to adapt and absorb local customs and beliefs was both key to their success and, later, the object of criticism by some Muslims.

Sufi orders have played an important role in Muslim societies. Frequently they included not only important scholars and philosophers but also government officials as well as charismatic individuals who challenged the legal and theological authorities. The latter often regarded Sufis with suspicion, seeing them as rivals to their own, more legalistic interpretations of Islam.

Being a Sufi does not exclude following the sharia, however. Indeed, Sufis would say that Sufi practice begins with mastery of the sharia. Some of the greatest names in Islam, including the poet Rumi and Abu Hamid Muhammad al-Ghazali (d. 1111), were both Sufis and experts in Islamic jurisprudence. Islam's most important theologian, al-Ghazali sought to show that the interior dimensions of Sufism and the external structure of the sharia reinforced each other and were both crucial for cultivating awareness of the divine.

Sufi convents existed for both men and women, with female Sufi circles tending to be more oriented to local shrines, and male associations more international. Sufi orders offered local communities a variety of spiritual and corporal services. The tombs of Sufi saints became a source of blessings to the population; the saint's *baraka* (grace) was transmitted to family members or associates, giving them curative or mediatory powers that enabled them to intercede for others and resolve physical, emotional, spiritual, and social problems. Sufi dhikr (remembrance) provided the community with an additional devotional liturgy that was dramatic, mystical, and emotional.

Sufis have encompassed a wide range of believers. What all Sufis hold in common is a belief that God can be known and experienced in this life, not just the next. Their emphasis on the mystical communion of love has had a wide influence on popular Islam but has sometimes been controversial. The practice of venerating Sufi saints and shrines has been criticized by some nineteenth- and twentieth-century Muslim reformers as superstitious and contrary to Islam. They blame Sufism for corrupting Islam and contributing to the political weakness of Islamic nations vis-à-vis European imperialism. Though Sufism has come under internal attack, it has become popular in some circles in the West, where it is seen as the tolerant face of Islam and a form of universal religion to which everyone can subscribe.

Today Sufism is still an influence among Muslims, part of Islam's enduring tradition, but its otherworldly orientation and emphasis on obedience to a spiritual master put it at variance with the temper of the times. In an era in which everyone wants to become successful, the spirit of Sufism still speaks, but not, perhaps, as powerfully as it did in an earlier age that was more oriented toward the life to come than to prosperity in this one. Just as Christian monastics in the West have trouble making their way of life seem compelling and relevant today, so, too, do Sufis.

WAHHABISM

Since the, attacks on the World Trade Center and the Pentagon on September 11, 2001, there has been increased awareness in this country of the Wahhabi movement in Islam. Many of the 9/11 hijackers were from Saudi Arabia, where the ultraconservative Wahhabi school of Sunni Islam provides the religious basis for the state and the society.

Wahhabism is a puritanical movement founded by the religious reformer Muhammad Ibn Abd al-Wahhab (1703–1791), who allied himself with the al-Saud family in the eighteenth century. Al-Wahhab viewed many popular beliefs and practices of his time as a reversion to pre-Islamic paganism and advocated a return to what he saw as the fundamentals of Islam. His particular brand of religious fervor helped unite a tribal coalition under the House of Saud and has been dominant in Saudi Arabia ever since.

The Wahhabis consider that any veneration of tombs or shrines is idolatrous and against the spirit of Muslim monotheism. Their opposition to these forms of Sufi and Shi'i spirituality has often taken destructive form. In 1801, Wahhabi forces destroyed the dome of the tomb of the Shi'i Imam Husayn in Karbala in what is now Iraq. Twenty-five years later, in 1826, Wahhabis destroyed the tombs of the family of Muhammad in Medina and even threatened to destroy the tomb of the Prophet Muhammad himself.

These acts created an antipathy between the Shi'is and the Wahhabis of Saudi Arabia that has endured up to the present day. The abolition of images and art, including Ottoman-era buildings in Saudi Arabia, has extended even to the occasional demand that family photographs in photo albums be destroyed. This iconoclastic impulse has continued to be a hallmark of Wahhabism. Comparisons have been made between Wahhabis and some Protestant reformers in Europe at the time of the Reformation who felt it necessary to destroy Catholic shrines and monasteries. People have also pointed to the Taliban's destruction of Buddhist monuments in Afghanistan in 2001, which was condemned by Muslim leaders around the world as Wahhabi-inspired.

The Wahhabis' strict literalism has led them to regard the text as the only legitimate source of Islam and to dismiss most of Islamic history as a degeneration of the true religion. Even the tradition of Islamic jurisprudence is regarded as a form of sophistry. Today when one hears many demands for Muslim modernization and reform, it is interesting to keep in mind the words of the great scholar of Islam Marshall Hodgson, who noted that "tradition is not the contrary of progress but the vehicle of it, and one of the problems of Muslims is that on the level of historical action their ties with relevant traditions are so tenuous" (*The Venture of Islam*, vol. 3, p. 431).

The Wahhabis' strain of religion is allied closely to the Salafist movement, which calls for adherence to the ways of the *salaf*, or "forebears," that is, the early companions of the Prophet. Founded in the late nineteenth century by such Muslim reformers as Muhammad Abduh and Jamal al-Din al-Afghani, the Salafists believed that Muslims should model themselves upon the Prophet and his companions and should reinterpret the original sources of Islam in light of modern needs, without being bound by the interpretations of earlier Muslim generations.

While the Salafists were more tolerant of diversity within Islam than the Wahhabis, they, too, had little interest in Islamic history after the time of Muhammad. Embracing egalitarianism, they promoted the idea that anyone could return to the original sources of Islam and discern the divine will. The Salafists were not anti-Western, however. Rather, they sought to identify democracy and socialism and the nation-state with Islam itself, locating within the Quran the roots of these contemporary philosophies and institutions.

Over time the modernist orientation that had initially characterized Salafism changed. Salafism came under the influence of Wahhabism, and the two became nearly indistinguishable. Indeed, Wahhabi clerics are more apt to identify themselves as Salafist than Wahhabi. Wahhabism (and contemporary Salafism) is sometimes accused of promoting a form of Islam that is puritanical, self-righteous, and arrogant, going beyond vindicating Islam's relevance and authority to insisting on Islam's superiority to other religions and to the West—this despite its being alienated from Islam's own heritage and traditions.

Saudi Arabia, a center of Wahhabism, is one of a handful of Islamic states that base their legitimacy on Islam and claim to be governed by Islamic law and the Quran. Other states in which Muslims live are either completely secular or are Muslim states, meaning that their system of modern constitutional government is based on that of the West, with the addition of some Islamic provisions, for instance requiring that the head of state be Muslim.

MISSION

Islam, the youngest of the three Abrahamic faiths to emerge, has historically been the most universalistic. Inspired by both Judaism and Christianity, it is in many respects closer to Judaism in having a sacred language and law and a strong iconoclastic bent. But whereas Jews have historically believed that they serve the world simply by providing an example to it, Muslims have traditionally understood themselves to have a universal responsibility to "command the right and forbid the wrong." Their obligation to God demanded that they bring what they believe to be God's revelation to the worldwide society in the creation of a social order enabling people to fulfill their God-given destiny. This responsibility was direct, personal, and all-embracing and applied to every person who embraced Islam. This is the basis of the egalitarianism of Islam. There are no priests in Islam because the duties of the faith apply equally to everyone. There are scholars of sharia who have a quasi-clerical function, especially in Shi'ism, but they do not act as intercessors between God and humankind.

Intimidating as their responsibility to act as God's agents on earth might appear, Muslims in the past traditionally leavened the temptation to arrogance by stressing moderation and balance. They were urged to balance faith and the affairs of the world. They were not to become so preoccupied with faith that they join a monastery and abandon the world; neither were they supposed to be so consumed by worldly cares and ambitions that they forgot God's preeminent place in the cosmos and in their heart. Similarly, prayer and family life were meant to be balanced. Sex was regarded as good but should be restricted to marriage. People were to enjoy food but to eat moderately and exercise.

From their religion, Muslims acquired a sense of historical mission. History was the arena in which Muslims were to live out their duty to God. But this sense of mission was not meant to make them exclusivist. Unlike Jews, Muslims did not regard themselves as unique, a chosen people singled out by God, not after the decision was made to reject Arabism as a basis for membership in the Muslim community. And unlike Christians, Muslims did not see their mission as excluding revelations made to other peoples. In the Muslim view, all of God's revelations were blessed at origin. Rather than criticize the messages that God has given to other peoples, the Quran suggests that Jews, Christians, and Muslims compete with each other in doing good deeds.

"To everyone of you we have given a rule and a beaten track. . . . And if God had pleased He had surely made you all one people; but He would test you by what He hath given to each. Be emulous, then, in good deeds. To God shall ye *all* return, and He will tell you concerning the subjects of your disputes" (Sura 5:52-53).

CHAPTER 3

Controversies and Misconceptions about Islam

ISLAM AND VIOLENCE

For reasons that have little to do with religion per se, Islam and the West in general and the United States in particular are increasingly at odds with each other today. There are complex geopolitical reasons for this, but one consequence is that in the United States Islam itself is sometimes blamed for the tensions that exist between Muslims and the West. A common accusation is that Islam is a religion of violence.

Not surprisingly, Muslims disagree. The Quran describes Islam as a religion of peace. The very word "Islam" is based on a root (*s-l-m*) that carries several meanings in Arabic: peace, safety, security, soundness, certainty, and salvation. This root is related to the Hebrew word *shalom*, meaning "peace," and peace is one of the attributes of God, the Quran says. Muhammad is quoted as saying "O God, you are peace and peace comes from you." Peace and greetings are closely intertwined in Islam; the Quran directs Muslims to greet others in peace as a sign of the peaceful relationship that should exist between them. Thus when Muslims meet and when they answer the phone, they say, "Peace be upon you."

To Muslims, peace connotes more than just the absence of war, however. It is a state of well-being encompassing all aspects of life in both the immediate present and in the hereafter. It is sometimes said that if the goal of Christianity is salvation, the goal of Islam is peace. Islam teaches that this peace must begin within the individual human heart before it can find expression in the external world. In *The Heart of Islam*, Seyyed Nossein Nasr writes, "For Islam, as for all authentic traditions, the goal of religion is to save the human soul and consequently establish justice and peace in society so that people can live virtuously and live and die 'in peace'" (pp. 220–21). If Muslims in the past described the world as divided into the Abode of Peace and the Abode of War (the Dar al-Islam being that part of the world governed by Muslims, and the Dar al-Harb those territories not ruled by Muslims), this was as much a theological and ontological concept as a political and military concern.

Mercy is another attribute of God, one constantly mentioned in the Quran. Despite its strong emphasis on the punishment that will be meted out to sinners and unbelievers, the Quran continually speaks of God as "the Merciful, the Compassionate." Mercy is one of the eternal attributes of God. God's mercy is a gift to believers in particular but extends to all of humanity regardless of belief.

Like Christianity, Islam teaches that those who want God's mercy must tender it to others. It praises the virtuous individual who returns good for evil and emphasizes that God's forgiveness is bountiful to all who want it. References to God's mercy proliferate in the Quran. "But to those who have done evil, then afterward repent and believe, thy Lord will thereafter be Lenient, Merciful" (Sura 7:152) is one such passage. In another, the Quran says, "Your Lord hath laid down for himself a law of mercy; so that if one of you commit a fault through ignorance, and afterwards turn and amend, He surely will be Gracious, Merciful" (Sura 6:54).

How, then, did Islam acquire a reputation as a warlike religion? There are many reasons. For one, many Christians know very little about Islam. Because Islam developed after Judaism and Christianity, and Muslims considered themselves heir to the best of both religions, they have historically known more about Christians than Christians have known about Muslims. Over the centuries Christians have been reluctant to recognize the claims of a younger, upstart religion and were often even unaware of what they were.

Aggravating the religious antagonism that led Christians to dismiss Muslims as heathens and heretics, and Muslims to regard Christians as belonging to a corrupted faith, Muslims and Christians vied for power on the world stage. Though these conflicts were—and are—essentially political, they were often described as religious wars, with religious arguments invoked to support them. It has only been in the last fifty years or so that Christians and Muslims have made much of an effort to enter into dialogue with one another, but even here efforts have often been more fitful than sustained. In the United States the study of Islam has lagged behind the study of other world religions, although that is changing dramatically now.

Some scholars find it ironic that after the past century, in which two world wars in Christian Europe killed millions of people, it is Muslims rather than Christians who are accused of violence. They observe that from 1798 to the end of World War I and the dismantling of the Ottoman Empire, it was Western powers that forcibly conquered and colonized Muslim countries, not the other way around. Nonetheless, some today are quick to accuse Muslims of being violent when the latter have far more often been the targets, rather than the initiators, of violence at the hands of the Christian West. In his book *Following Muhammad: Rethinking Islam in the Contemporary World*, Professor Carl Ernst notes the prevalence of anti-Islamic stereotypes in the West and speculates that a kind of psychological projection is at work in which the West's own negative characteristics are projected onto the Muslim world (p. 30).

Whatever the truth of this statement, those who claim that Islam is a suspect and violent religion denounce the militancy of those Muslims who believe that the only way for Muslims to advance socially, politically, and economically today is to vigorously embrace their faith in the face of the overwhelming dominance of Western values. Such Muslims do not speak for the entire

Muslim population, yet they are sometimes depicted by Western detractors as representative of all Muslims. Often these Western commentators offer a misleading picture of Islam as a one-dimensional, univocal force without the divisions and diversity found in their own Christian or Jewish faith. They inveigh against Muslim fundamentalism as if it were uniquely dangerous while failing to mention that fundamentalism is on the rise in many religions, including Judaism, Christianity, and Hinduism.

Many such critics of Islam point to passages in the Quran that they say condone or counsel violence in self-defense. Such passages do exist, just as there are passages in the Jewish and Christian Scriptures that speak of taking violent measures against one's enemies. In Matthew 10:34, Jesus says: "Do not think that I have come to bring peace on earth. I have not come to bring peace, but a sword." In the Hebrew Scriptures there are the chilling verses: "When I whet my flashing sword, and my hand takes hold on judgment, I will take vengeance on my adversaries, and will repay those who hate me. I will make my arrows drunk with blood, and my sword shall devour flesh—with the blood of the slain and the captives, from the long-haired enemy" (Deut 32:42-43).

Like the Bible, the Quran is open to multiple interpretations, for it is alternately martial and peaceful, tolerant and stern, admonitory and forgiving. In one passage it says, "Believers! Wage war against such of the infidels as are your neighbors, and let them find you rigorous: and know that God is with those who fear him (Sura 9:123). In another it warns against zealotry and counsels Muslims to "fight for the cause of God against those who fight against you, but commit not the injustice of attacking them first for God loveth not such injustice" (Sura 2:186). The Quran prohibits aggressive war and counsels the merciful treatment of captives.

JIHAD

The much-misunderstood Muslim concept of *jihad*, or struggle, is often cited as support for the view that Islam is a warlike religion. The struggle can refer to the interior effort to be virtuous (the greater jihad) or to a physical struggle to defend Islam against aggression (the lesser jihad) or to the struggle against injustice and oppression. Jihad connotes the willingness to give up all, including one's life, for the sake of God.

Frequently Westerners decry the concept of jihad, which they often erroneously translate as "holy war," ignoring or perhaps unaware that holy war is a concept with roots in the Judeo-Christian tradition. The most famous example is the Crusades, which were initiated by the Christian West in order to capture the Holy Land. While the Christian rulers and merchants who went to war often did so for political and military reasons, in the hope of economic and commercial rewards, religious zeal was undoubtedly a prime motive for many of the foot soldiers of the Crusades. Rallying Christians in 1095 for the first Crusade, Pope Urban II offered absolution of sin to those who took part in it. "Let this then be your war cry in combats, because it is given to you by God. When an armed attack is made upon the enemy, let this one cry be raised by all the soldiers of God: 'It is the will of God! It is the will of God!'" (*Speech at the Council of Clermont*).

Though many religions have some version of a holy war—what Americans today would term a "just war" and Muslims would call the "lesser jihad"—the struggle for self-mastery and self-perfection, that is, the greater jihad, is intrinsic to most spiritual and religious traditions, including Christianity. Like Muslims, Christians are also asked to contend with their selfish desires. There are numerous passages in the New Testament that use striking metaphors to express the battle that believers must wage against their baser instincts: "If your right eye causes you to sin, tear it out and throw it away; it is better for you to lose one of your members than for your whole body to be thrown into hell. And if your right hand causes you to sin, cut it off and throw it away" (Matthew 5:29-30).

Similarly, St. Paul, in his letter to the Ephesians, counsels: "Put on the whole armor of God, so that you may be able to stand against the wiles of the devil. For our struggle is not against enemies of blood and flesh, but against the rulers, against the authorities, against the cosmic powers of this present darkness, against the spiritual forces of evil in the heavenly places. Therefore take up the whole armor of God, so that you may be able to withstand on that evil day, and having done everything, to stand firm" (6:11-13).

After the bitter wars of religion between Protestants and Catholics in Europe, the idea of a holy war, a war fought for religion, lost its currency in the Christian West. Except in some poorer countries, the concept of a holy war was replaced by the idea of a just war. In today's secular society in the United States, the rousing language of war is not uncommonly applied to social ills. Thus we have the war on poverty and the war on drugs. When war becomes not just a metaphor for a worthy campaign but an actuality, political leaders of all religious persuasions and in every culture typically assure their citizens marching off to battle that they are engaged in a noble enterprise. American leaders routinely invoke civil religion and the language of freedom and democracy to justify foreign conflicts. Thus all wars are described as wars to advance freedom and democracy, regardless of whether they are or not. Because noble goals are attributed to them, they are seen as righteous and sanctified.

For Muslims in modern times, the lesser jihad has a connotation similar to what those in the West would call a just war. The debate in the United States and throughout the world over the war in Iraq underscores how people can and do disagree over what is and is not a just war. For many, the United States-led invasion of Iraq in 2003 was an act of unprovoked aggression. Others attributed noble motives to United States leaders, despite the failure to discover weapons of mass destruction in Iraq, the supposed existence of which furnished the pretext for the war.

Jihad, encompassing both the greater and lesser forms, has deep roots in the Islamic tradition. From the outset Muhammad and his followers had to fight for their faith. The Muslims triumphed in Medina through a combination of military force, shrewd diplomacy, and popular enthusiasm, and this has colored Muslims attitudes since. Because it provided them legitimacy, for centuries dynastic rulers often self-servingly appropriated the word "jihad" to describe their wars against various opponents. Under the empire of the early caliphate, any war on a non-Muslim realm was called jihad (Ernst, *Following Muhammad*, p. 118).

Some jurists supported an interpretation of jihad as a religious duty for Muslims to conquer the world. Other scholars disagreed, saying that war could be undertaken only in self-defense. The most radical interpretation of the lesser jihad, or the jihad of the sword, has often been used by Europeans and Americans to argue that Muslims are inclined to wage war on non-Muslims as part of their religion. That many Muslims would object to the use of violence to spread Islam as contrary to the spirit of the religion is discounted, as if only the most radical version of Islam can be authentically Islam.

Unlike in the Catholic Church, however, there is no central authority, no magisterium, that speaks for Islam or can represent it authoritatively. Jihad can mean any number of things to any number of people. Jihad may mean defending one's country; it may also mean helping the poor or seeking knowledge. Muslim extremists sometimes use the word to justify the violent actions they undertake, even though the murder of innocent people is not condoned by the Quran or Islamic law and is considered by most Muslims a flagrant misuse of their religion.

Determining the legitimate and illegitimate use of violence is a question that extends far beyond the borders of the Muslim world. From Basque separatists in Spain, to Protestant paramilitaries and the Catholic IRA in Northern Ireland, to the Hindu Tamil Tigers in Sri Lanka, people of all religions, races, and ethnicities have taken up armed struggle on behalf of a cause that they feel justifies violence. Resistance movements, liberation movements, terrorism—the choice of terminology often depends on a person's point of view and whether he or she views the movement's aims and actions as defensive or aggressive.

Christianity is not a pacifist religion, and both international law and the tenets of most Christian churches accept that people have a right to defend themselves against aggression. When the

United States armed the mujahidin in Afghanistan to fight the Soviet Union in the 1980s, United States officials called them "freedom fighters." That many of those "freedom fighters" then became "terrorists" may say more about how political interests and allegiances change than about the character of those who took up arms against the Soviet Union when it invaded and, later, against the United States.

Reconciling one's religious obligations as a faithful Muslim, Christian, or Jew with the demands of the community and state can be a complex issue that does not lend itself to easy answers. Were the American colonists who broke with the British crown fighting a just war by Christian standards? The American Revolution was a political war, yet those fighting it on either side often drew on the language of religion to justify their cause. How we view a political issue is likely to depend on any number of factors; important among these are moral values influenced by our religion and culture.

MUHAMMAD

Another controversy arises over Western depictions of Muhammad. After his first wife, Khadija, died, the Prophet took other wives. Many of his wives were widows to whom he extended protection by marrying. Some marriages seem to have been entered into for reasons of state. His youngest wife, A'isha, was the daughter of his companion Abu Bakr, who succeeded Muhammad as the leader of the Islamic community. A'isha outlived Muhammad and became one of the most important sources of information about the Prophet.

Muhammad's multiple marriages have led Christians to portray him as a sensualist. Muslims have often felt highly insulted by such depictions. The issue of Muhammad's marriages speaks to different perspectives on sexuality in Christianity and Islam. Celibacy has been valued in the Christian, and specifically the Catholic, tradition, but it is not promoted in Islam. Celibacy is one reason why Muslims sometimes see Christianity as advocating an impossible ideal, whereas they see their own faith as more practicable for everyday life.

Because he was both a political and a religious leader, Muhammad is more akin to Moses or to David in the Old Testament than to Jesus. Christians have tended to consider Muhammad insufficiently spiritual and have faulted him for possessing political ambitions and for leading his people into battle. Though the model of sacrificial nonviolence that Jesus provided has not resulted in Christians' being appreciably more pacifist than followers of other major religions, it has established an ideal that Christians disparage Muhammad for not reflecting. His martial prowess and his multiple marriages—in all, Muhammad had ten wives after Khadija and two concubines—are marks against him in the eyes of Christians. Conversely, Muslims have found Christians' admiration of pacifism and celibacy unrealistic and ultimately hypocritical. Christians are seen as giving lip service to ideals they make little attempt to practice.

Often Christians have perceived as defects the very qualities Muslims have revered in Muhammad. Muslim tradition has it that Muhammad was illiterate. While Muslims have seen this as evidence of the divine origin of the Quran, Christians have treated it as proof of Muhammad's fraudulence. Muslims see the fact that Muhammad claimed the Quran as his only miracle as evidence of the spirituality of his mission; Christians have regarded it as corroboration that he was not a true prophet. These antithetical views of Muhammad persisted for centuries, with Muhammad variously portrayed by Christians as a Christian renegade, a schismatic, and sometimes the anti-Christ himself. Dante placed Muhammad in the eighth circle of hell; Luther saw him as one of the two archenemies of Christ along with the pope.

In contrast, for Muslims Muhammad represents the well-balanced individual, one who reflects human personality in combining both an inward, contemplative nature and an extroverted ability to lead others. If innumerable hadiths report what Muhammad said and did, it is because he is a model of faithful living. Muhammad is "the living Quran," whose sincerity, piety, gentleness, and compassion can inspire others to similar behavior.

THE STATUS OF WOMEN

Gender relations have been another controversial issue between Muslims and Westerners. Islam is commonly perceived in the West as a patriarchal and misogynistic religion that oppresses women. Westerners tend to plume themselves on their superior tolerance and egalitarianism in this respect, which ironically they then use to buttress their belief in their own superiority. They seldom look at the evolution of gender relations in Western societies or at the ambiguous record of Christianity on this matter. Like Islam, Christianity can be said to have elevated the status of women in the countries in which it took root. Like Islam, Christianity has also been accused of being a patriarchal religion that does not place equal value on the contributions of women. In both religions the fairness of such accusations is contested.

The Quran's statements about women can be cited to both support and refute claims that Islam privileges men over women. On one hand, there are passages in the Quran that clearly indicate that men and women enjoy the same spiritual rewards and are spiritual equals before the Lord. "But whoso doth the things that are right, whether male or female, and he or she is a believer—these shall enter Paradise" (Sura 4:123). Another chapter in the Quran elaborates on this in very gender-specific language: "Truly the men who resign themselves to God (Muslims), and the women who resign themselves, and the believing men and the believing women, and the devout men and the devout women, and the men of truth, and the women of truth, and the patient men and the patient women, and the humble men and the humble women, and the men who give alms and the women who give alms, and the men who fast and the women who fast, and the chaste men and the chaste women, and the men and the women who oft remember God: for them hath God prepared forgiveness and a rich recompense" (Sura 33:35).

There are other statements in the Quran that indicate that men are regarded as the natural leaders of the community. The Quran states that two men or one man and two women are necessary to witness a legal transaction. "Men are superior to women on account of the qualities with which God has gifted the one above the other, and on account of the outlay they make for their substance from them" (Sura 4:38). Christians might compare this to St. Paul's statement that women are to be subject to their husbands as to the Lord (Ephesians 5:21).

Muslim feminists often make the point that it is not Muhammad and the Quran that should be held accountable for Muslim women's inferior status in many Muslim societies, but the local, male-dominated tribal cultures in which Islam often took root. Indeed, in most parts of the world, women were for centuries held in low esteem, whether in the East or the West. In Ancient Greece women were always under the control of their husbands, fathers, or brothers and had few if any rights. Their consent to marriage was rarely sought, and their inferiority to men was assumed. Women fared little better in Ancient Rome, though Rome is often credited with bringing law and good government to the societies it ruled. The Old Testament is full of heroic women, but it also contains many stories of women who were given as sexual chattel. In most Western societies women's emancipation is of relatively recent origin. The struggle for women's rights occurred in the last century and a half, with women not receiving the vote in most countries until the twentieth century. Even today the wages men and women earn in many, if not most, Western societies are unequal, and careers dominated by men are better paid than careers populated largely by women.

In Muslim societies today, the status of women varies widely. In conservative Saudi Arabia, women are not allowed to drive cars, must completely cover themselves in public, and are strictly segregated from men. In Malaysia, women ride motorcycles to work or school, hold responsible jobs in every field of activity, and have the same access to education as men, but they must often seek their father's or brother's permission if they want to travel outside the country. Women have served as prime ministers in Bangladesh, Pakistan, and Turkey and as president of Indonesia, yet women in those countries also face curbs on their freedom that would strike many Western women as onerous.

Often, even within the same society, conditions for women vary enormously, depending on whether a woman is living in the countryside or the city. And even in countries where women are severely restricted in what they can and cannot do, their status usually entails more complexity than Westerners perceive. For instance, Saudi women own their own businesses, are large landowners, and attend university in greater numbers than do Saudi men.

Today many Muslim women around the world are feeling a greater sense of empowerment and are vigorously engaging in the public debate on a range of issues, including the role of women in Islam. Some argue for greater freedom for women on the basis of the Quran itself, which they say has been misinterpreted by men; some argue for women's rights from within the tradition of Islamic jurisprudence. In general, Muslim feminists accept neither the Western proposition that Islam is inherently prejudicial against women nor the view held by some conservative Muslim men that women should subordinate themselves to men. They reject forms of Western women's liberation judged to be incompatible with Islam and advocate for a more egalitarian social order that does not necessarily reject traditional gender roles but emphasizes flexibility and informed consent on the part of women (Denny, *Introduction to Islam*, p. 354).

THE VEIL

The veil has become a fraught subject between Muslims and Westerners. The latter often see the practice of women covering themselves with a veil as a symbol of oppression. In Afghanistan the puritanical Taliban regime forced women to cover themselves completely and denied them jobs and education in the name of Islam. The burqa, the shroud-like garment with slits for the wearer's eyes that women were forced to wear in Afghanistan, came to

be seen as an apt metaphor for the Taliban's effort to stifle wom-
en's opportunities and creative potential.

Other Muslim women have not been forced by their fathers
or brothers to wear the veil but have put it on either as a mark of
freely chosen religious observance or, sometimes, as a gesture of
defiance against Western cultural and political dominance. The
Quran does not elaborate on the issue of how women should
dress. Muhammad's wives wore veils as a mark of distinction, as
did other upper-class women, but the practice of veiling only became widespread in the Islamic empire several generations after
Muhammad's death. Even then most women in the countryside
did not wear veils.

Those who insist that women cover themselves refer to a passage in the Quran that tells believers how they should comport
themselves when they are in Muhammad's household. Interpreters discuss this passage in terms of the multiple demands
that were placed on Muhammad when he became the leader of
Medina and the number of people who streamed in and out of
his quarters, annoying his wives with their constant presence
and demands. The Quran reads: "And when ye would ask any
gift of his wives, ask it from behind a veil. Purer will this be for
your hearts and for their hearts" (Sura 33:53).

Another chapter in the Quran directs men and women to
dress modestly and contains a brief, vague reference to veils:

> Speak unto the believers that they restrain their eyes and ob-
> serve continence. Thus will they be more pure. God is well aware
> of what they do. . . . And speak to the believing women that
> they refrain their eyes and observe continence; and that they dis-
> play not their ornaments, except those which are external; and
> that they throw their veils over their bosoms, and display not
> their ornaments, except to their husbands and fathers, or their
> husbands' fathers or their sons, or their husbands' sons or their
> brothers (Sura 24:30-31).

Most Muslim women today do not wear any kind of head
covering at all. Some wear loose, flowing garments that cover

everything but their face or hands. Still other women wear just a headscarf, or *hijab*, that covers their hair but leaves their face bare.

Westerners frequently view Muslim women who cover their heads as oppressed, even though women in many different countries and cultures do the same. Catholic nuns, Amish women, Russian, Greek, Jewish women, and others have worn veils or head scarves. Many continue to do so, yet are not automatically assumed to be subservient because of it. Muslim women sometimes resent the insinuation that Muslim women's head coverings and dress make them inferior to or weaker than Western women. To those who say that Western women are freer because they enjoy self-expression in how they dress and wear their hair, some Muslim women respond that Western women only think they are freer because they are unconscious of how much effort and money they are putting into appealing to men by wearing uncomfortable high heels and tight skirts. Women who allow themselves to be used as sex objects in advertisements and commercials or in their day-to-day life have neither freedom nor dignity, they assert.

Advocates for veils or simply loose clothing for women say it dignifies women by focusing on their personhood rather than their sex. Veiling minimizes the importance attached to physical attractiveness, thus enabling women to have healthier self-esteem. It frees a woman to concentrate on her studies and professional skills, with less concern for how she appears to males and their possible sexual interest or rejection, and it minimizes sexual competition with other women. In the same way, habits for nuns were said to give nuns freedom from sex roles. Whether wearing a veil really has this effect no doubt depends on any number of specific circumstances. Moreover, even women who are veiled find ways to enhance their attractiveness to the opposite sex. Opponents of veiling insist that even if it is true that the veil frees women from unwelcome male attention, women's behavior should not be curtailed by the conduct of men. Women's freedom should not be more restricted than men's.

The question of veiling, like the status of women, is complicated, in part because it touches on cultural mores that have less
to do with Islam per se than it does with the role of custom
and the impact of modernization on traditional and sometimes
tribal societies. Some Muslim men do insist that their wives and
daughters wear a veil. There are also cases in which women have
insisted on veiling themselves despite the opposition of their
family. Some Western women who have converted to Islam say
that wearing a head covering gives them a greater feeling of freedom and dignity; they feel they are no longer looked at chiefly in
terms of their sexual attractiveness.

TOLERANCE

A common critique of Islam is that it is not a religion of tolerance. Historically, this is untrue. There was no general Inquisition that operated in Muslim countries, and forced conversion,
persecution, and expulsion were the exception, not the rule. In
exchange for paying a special tax, religious minorities under
Muslim rule were allowed to practice their religion and to live
according to their own religious law with a minimum of inter-
ference. Contrary to stereotypes, Islam was not typically spread
by the sword. Indeed, because Islamic rulers received extra taxes
from religious minorities, they were initially reluctant to wel-
come converts because of the revenue they would forego. Though
Islamic jurisdiction often spread through war, the purpose of the
warfare was not to force individual conversion. Islam also spread
peacefully, especially through trade, into Africa, Indonesia, and
the Philippines.

It is true that in the twenty-first century many Muslim societies are far more traditional than those in the West. Gender
roles tend to be more rigidly defined; the process of secularization has not advanced as rapidly; customs and mores tend to be
stricter. For these reasons, many Americans regard Muslims as
intolerant and backward. Many Muslims, on the other hand, are
shocked by what they regard as Western materialism and licen-

tiousness—the easy availability of pornography, sexually explicit imagery in commercials and popular entertainment, the acceptance of greed as the chief motive force in people's lives.

MARTYRDOM

Frequent suicide bombings in Palestine, Iraq, and elsewhere have led Westerners to think that Muslims have an aberrant, inexplicable suicide complex particular to their culture. However, martyrdom has a long tradition in both Christianity and Islam. The early Christians who were martyred for their faith were Christianity's first saints; martyrs who die in defense of Islamic ideals are also venerated in Islam, where sacrificial death is considered the ultimate witness to God. The Arabic word for martyr is *shahid*, meaning "witness," and is related to the *shahada*, the confession of witness.

The Quran contains several passages praising the worthiness of those who give up their lives in defense of Islam. "And if ye shall be slain or die on the path of God, then pardon from God and mercy is better than all your amassings. For if ye die or be slain, verily unto God shall ye be gathered" (Sura 3:151-152). In the same chapter the Quran later says: "And repute not those slain on God's path to be dead. Nay, alive with their Lord, are they richly sustained" (Sura 3:163).

The stories about Muhammad reported in the hadith also speak of the graces that will come to those who die in defense of Islam. Their sacrifice frees them from sin, and they do not undergo the postmortem interrogations of the angels Nakir and Munkar, who confront the dead with the good and bad deeds they've committed; such martyrs do not experience purgatory but go directly to heaven. Because of the state of purity in which they died, their bodies are not washed, as is usually done to the dead, and they are buried in the clothes they were martyred in.

While martyrdom is admired in Islam, suicide is not. As in Catholicism, suicide is prohibited as a moral evil. Muslims in battle are enjoined to struggle to survive rather than ever to choose death. Islamic jurisprudence demands three conditions for martyrdom: There must be a state of war; there must be a chance that the individual taking on what would seem a hopeless, suicidal mission will survive; death must come from his adversary (Capan, *Terror and Suicide Attacks*, p. 96). Nonetheless, both Sunni and Shi'i Muslims venerate those who die in the cause of jihad. Those who die defending certain basic rights, such as the right to life, property, home, and family, are also considered martyrs.

Shi'i Islam has a particularly rich tradition of martyrdom stemming from the slaughter of Muhammad's grandson Husayn and his followers on the plains of Karbala in 680 by the army of the Sunni caliph Yazid. Every year people make pilgrimage to the graves of those martyrs, and Husayn's sacrificial death is re-enacted with lamentations and prayers by the Shi'i community.

The tradition of martyrdom has broadened in recent decades. Soldiers in wars against colonial powers were called martyrs, and both sides in the Iran-Iraq war (1980–1988) described their slain soldiers as martyrs. Palestinians also regularly describe men, women, or children killed by Israeli soldiers as martyrs.

Whether suicide bombers can be called martyrs is debatable. Obviously, suicide bombers consider their acts justifiable, or they would not be doing them. Those who defend such attacks usually claim that the opposing side possesses overwhelming advantages in terms of weapons, numbers, logistical support, military support, and support from the media. In some cases the deaths of suicide bombers are described as incidental rather than purposive—hence not suicide—an unfortunate corollary to an act of violence they present as self-defense.

However, even if one accepts the argument that suicide bombers are attempting to protect their society from a ruthless enemy that possesses far greater advantage, the Quran says clearly that one injustice does not excuse another. Moreover, Islamic law forbids the killing of civilians in wartime, much less in times of peace. The deliberate murder of another human being ranks with shirk (idolotry) as the worst sin a Muslim can commit. Thus most Muslim religious and legal scholars have condemned suicide bombings as unjustifiable and un-Islamic. The September 11 attacks were widely condemned by Muslims. The attacks on London's subways in July 2005 were also condemned by numerous Muslim groups as antithetical to the teachings of Islam. But not all Muslim scholars support sweeping condemnations of suicide attacks. Some have said that such attacks can be justified as acts of resistance.

Suicide attacks are not unique to Muslim culture. As the fortunes of war turned in favor of the United States during World War II, an increasingly desperate Japan mounted kamikaze attacks against United States ships. Beginning in 1987, the Tamil Tigers in Sri Lanka, a secular Hindu national liberation group, embraced suicide attacks as a way to press their campaign for independence from Sri Lanka.

Suicide attacks almost always take place in the context of warfare in which one side has much greater military resources than the other. Rather than regarding suicide bombing as evidence of barbarism, it is probably more accurate to see such attacks as a feature of modern political violence that prioritizes an ideology or cause as being more important than life itself (Mamdani, *Good Muslim, Bad Muslim*, p. 222). Patrick Henry's famous statement "Give me liberty or give me death" during the American Revolution is one that revolutionaries of all kinds, including suicide bombers, would endorse.

Recent research indicates that suicide attacks tend to take place in the context of foreign occupation, often against an occupier of a different religion. Suicide attacks are not common in Muslim societies. For instance, suicide bombings were not prevalent in Iraq prior to the 2003 United States invasion.

MODERNIZATION

Western critics of Islam sometimes describe it as authoritarian, anti-democratic, and ill-adapted to the modern world. Its defenders argue that there is a strong tradition of pluralism within Islam that makes it supportive of democracy. Islam acknowledges multiple sources of revelation; it endorses the role of community consensus in making decisions; legal concepts such as ijtihad (independent reasoning) lend themselves to democracy. They also point out that since it comes from a different tradition, Islamic democracy will probably not duplicate—nor does it need to—Western democracy but will develop its own authentic way. Many Muslims draw a strong distinction between modernization, which they support, and Westernization, which they disavow.

The issue of modernization is sometimes presented in an illusory either-or way. Often the comment is made that Muslims must choose between modernization and Mecca, as if religion and modernization were inherently at odds or as if Islam were somehow more inherently unsuited to modernity than Judaism or Christianity. But there are millions of observant middle-class Muslims who drive cars to work, watch satellite TV, work on computers, use cell phones and faxes, and travel by jet plane. Modern technology is fully integrated into their lives, and this is no more a problem for them than it is for most twenty-first-century Americans.

To the degree that modernity involves secularization and a reduction of religion to the private sphere, that is an issue for people of all faith traditions. Because Islam from its inception was both a religion and a political regime that strove to create a righteous society in which people could serve God, the division between religion and state that has developed in modern Western states is difficult for some Muslims today to endorse, but this is a matter of degree more than kind.

For countless generations Muslims have lived in an imperfect world, the political realities of which did not comport with the ideals of their faith. If Muslims today struggle to balance principles and pragmatism, so, too, do Christians and Jews, many of whom are uneasy about a purely privatized religion. Islam's traditional emphasis on being a "middle way," a balanced community that steers between extremes, may be a hopeful omen for Muslims' ability to reconcile the inevitable tension between faith and politics.

Those critics who deplore Islam's failure to wall off religion from politics should keep in mind that after Emperor Theodosius I established Christianity as the official state religion, there was no separation of church and state in Christian nations until after the Enlightenment. Even today some European monarchs are heads of their national churches. Christians can quote the gospel as it relates to rendering unto Caesar what is Caesar's and giving to God what is God's, but deciding what belongs to Caesar and what belongs to God took more than a thousand years of messy feuding between church and state. It continues in various forms today: witness the struggles in this country over such issues as abortion, school prayer, stem cell research, evolution, and assisted suicide. Even in a system of government where church and state are kept separate, religious issues and interest groups continue to play a major role in setting the terms of political debate.

SECULARIZATION

Christians and Jews in the West live in secularized societies in which most people have a stronger allegiance to their country than to their religion. However, in many parts of the world where the nation-state is of more recent origin, people continue to derive their sense of identity less from their nationality than from their religion. While most Muslim-majority countries are headed by modern secular governments today, in some of them a strong sense of national allegiance has yet to take firm hold. Not surprisingly, efforts to secularize society that go against people's loyalties often create resistance.

More relevant perhaps to many Muslims' suspicions of secularization is a history of governments ruthlessly imposing secularization on an unwilling public. Despite episodes in Western history where religion was brutally repressed, secularization in the West is often perceived as a relatively benign process that evolved over time and reflected the popular will. It has been seen as guaranteeing religious freedom and enabling religion to concentrate on its spiritual ideals.

In many Muslim countries, the process has been far more trau-
matic and coercive. In the 1920s the Turkish leader Attaturk,
determined to build a modern state in Turkey after the collapse of
the Ottoman Empire, suppressed the *madrasas* (religious schools),
abolished Sufi orders, mandated a Latin alphabet instead of
Arabic, imposed Western surnames in place of old Islamic names
and titles, and forced Turks to wear Western dress. Reza Shah
Pahlavi, the shah of Iran who ruled from 1921 to 1941, stripped
the ulama, the religious scholars, of their endowment, replaced
the sharia with a civil-law code, prohibited citizens from going
on the hajj, suppressed the Shi'i religious rites commemorating
the death of Husayn, and forbade Islamic dress. His soldiers
tore off women's veils in the street, and unarmed protesters who
demonstrated against the regime's dress laws in 1935 were shot.
Hundreds died. His son Muhammad Reza Shah (1944–1979)
was just as anti-religious. He closed madrasas, restricted public
displays of religion, and imprisoned, exiled, and killed many
members of the ulama.

Because of these experiences, secularism is perceived by many
Muslims as anti-religious and intolerant and a threat to the
foundations of their society. Modernizing governments in the
past and in the present continue to see religion as an obstacle to
progress. How this tension will be resolved remains to be seen
and will almost certainly vary from country to country. But fig-
uring out how faith can be lived in the modern era is a task for
Muslims, Jews, and Christians alike. In all societies this is a work
in progress.

CHAPTER 4

Interfaith Relations between Islam, Christianity, and Judaism

Judaism, Christianity, and Islam are called the three Abrahamic faiths because they all claim descent from Abraham and share a belief in one God, a God who is active in human affairs, has revealed himself to humankind via a sacred Scripture, and has made a special covenant with his people. Americans and Europeans are used to thinking of Judaism and Christianity as Western religions and Islam as a Middle Eastern or even Oriental religion, but all three were born in what is called either the Near East or the Middle East. Despite the divisions drawn today, for centuries Jews and Christians lived in Muslim lands, participated with Muslims in a common culture, and were little different from their Muslim neighbors in their language, dress, mores, and manners (Peters, *Islam*, p. xii).

Developing in a polytheistic world, early monotheistic religions saw polytheism as their chief adversary and reserved their harshest censures for paganism. But as polytheism faded, monotheistic religions became more intolerant of one another as they vied for believers. While Judaism, Christianity, and Islam all emphasize moral responsibility for one's actions and reflect similar religious ideas, they drew distinctions between one and the other that came to be perceived as increasingly significant as time went by.

Tensions between the three faiths waned and waxed depending on the historical time period. For centuries Christian-Jewish relations were poisoned by mutual acrimony and the ugly history of Christian bigotry that made Jews, a minority population in Christian Europe, a frequent target for persecution. Notwithstanding Christian belief that the death of Jesus was necessary for the salvation of the world, Christians frequently held Jews responsible for the murder of Jesus. Jews were expelled from England in 1290, from Spain in 1492, and were periodically subjected to pogroms in Eastern Europe and Russia. As a minority population, Jews had few means to defend themselves and concentrated most of their energies on keeping their community together. They possessed their own polemic against Christianity, which focused on discrediting Jesus as the Messiah and showing him in an unflattering light.

The rise of the nation-state in Europe created new prejudice against Jews, based not on religious grounds but on economic, political, and social motives. In an increasingly nationalistic Europe, Jews were seen as outsiders and were accused of being a cosmopolitan elite with undeserved power and privilege. Following the murder of millions of Jews by Nazi Germany in the Second World War, Christian churches attempted to make amends for their role in contributing to anti-Semitism by promoting interfaith dialogue between Christians and Jews, emphasizing Jesus' Jewish roots, supporting the establishment of Israel as a Jewish state, and concentrating on the shared values of Judaism and Christianity. Whereas Jews living in Europe had earlier been seen as the "other" by the majority Christian population, the phrase "Judeo-Christian civilization" became current.

The relationship between Christianity and Islam and between Judaism and Islam is no less complex than the Christian-Jewish relationship. Each possesses its own particular history, grievances, and challenges.

CHRISTIAN-MUSLIM RIVALRY

Early contact between Christians and Muslims was infrequent but not unfriendly. As mentioned in a previous chapter (p. 3), one of Muhammad's first supporters was either a Christian or a hanif (pre-Islamic monotheist). At a time when Muhammad was troubled by how to interpret his visions, Waraqa ibn Nawful, the cousin of Muhammad's wife Khadija, encouraged him to take his prophetic vocation seriously. Five years after Muhammad first began to receive revelations from God, pressure on the new Muslims in Mecca was so severe that about a hundred of them moved to the Christian country of Ethiopia, where they were warmly received.

A charming hadith recounts how a Christian monk who met Muhammad early in his life recognized his gifts long before Muhammad had any idea of them. Muhammad was traveling to Syria for his then-employer, Khadija, when he and Khadija's slave Maysarah stopped near the home of Bahira, a Christian monk. The Prophet was sitting under a tree when Bahira came up to Maysarah and asked him about his companion. Maysara told him that Muhammad was one of the Quraysh, the tribe that guarded the Kaaba. The monk shook his head in wonder. "No one but a prophet is sitting beneath this tree," he said (Ahmed, *Islam Today*, p. 15).

Muhammad's positive feelings about Christians can be surmised from a verse in the Quran in which he says that Christians are closest to Muslims. "This because some of them are priests and monks, and because they are free from pride" (Sura 5:85).

Notwithstanding this promising beginning, tensions arose between Christians and Muslims. Unlike Judaism, a kinship-based religion that accepts but does not seek converts, both Christianity and Islam endeavor to proclaim their message to the world. Islam offered an alternative religious and political vision to Christianity, and perhaps inevitably members of the two religions saw themselves as rivals despite their similarities. If Christians saw their own covenant with God as superseding that of God's covenant with Israel and excluding later revelations,

Muslims believed that God's revelation to Muhammad corrected the corruption into which his earlier messages to the Jews and Christians had fallen. The earlier revelations were just as valid and significant, but the people to whom they had been given had failed to honor them properly. By regarding Jesus as divine, for instance, Muslims thought Christians had committed *shirk*, the worst sin in Islam. For their part, Christians were reluctant to concede any merit to an upstart religion that challenged its claim to exclusive truth. Moreover, the remarkable expansion of Islam, and the swift inroads it was able to make into the Byzantine Empire, meant that Islam threatened the political hegemony of Christendom.

It should be noted that Islam did not threaten Christian worship or belief so much as it did Christian political power. Islam may have united the Arab tribes, but the Arab conquest in the first few centuries after the death of Mohammad was political, not religious, in nature. Christian Arabs shared in the spoils of victory along with Muslims. While pagan practices were prohibited on pain of death, Jews and Christians and, later, Zoroastrians and Hindus were allowed to continue practicing their faith, and the stretched-thin conquering armies usually co-opted the governmental bureaucracies that existed.

Unlike some of history's brutal conquerors, the Arab armies did not practice indiscriminate pillaging. Arab warriors issued diplomatic ultimatums before they launched military invasions, enabling local princes to keep their head and their jobs in exchange for allegiance and tribute. The relatively generous terms accorded subject peoples meant that many local Christians often ended up preferring their Muslim conquerors to their former Christian overlords. For instance, in the Byzantine Empire some Christian groups that were persecuted by the official church welcomed Muslim rule, which imposed lighter taxes and proved more tolerant than imperial Christianity in according religious freedom to indigenous Christian churches and Jews.

Though many Christians and Jews under Islamic rule did end up becoming Muslims either for political and economic advantage or because they were genuinely persuaded by Islam's claims, this happened after Islam's conquest of Christian territories and not because of it. Though in history there are exceptions to every rule, Muslims generally did not force the local populations they conquered to convert to Islam. This was in keeping with the statement in the Quran: "Let there be no compulsion in Religion" (Sura 2:257).

Some scholars have described three periods in the Christian-Muslim relationship: an age of ignorance, from the birth of Islam to the twelfth century, in which the West largely ignored the reality of Islam; increased contact with Muslim societies starting in the twelfth century, leading to a more accurate understanding of Islam, during which time the Quran was translated into Latin and Islamic science and philosophy were introduced into European curricula, thereby commanding the admiration of some Christians; a third period following the fall of Constantinople to the Turks in 1453 (Anawati, in Ellis, *The Vatican, Islam and the Middle East*, p. 52).

If earlier, Christians had hoped to convert Muslims or defeat them on the battlefield, some Europeans began to advocate a more peaceful, realistic accommodation with them. The Catholic Church, which saw Islam as denying its essential doctrines and seeking to supplant it, vigorously condemned Islam. But from the Renaissance on, and particularly from the nineteenth century, increasing numbers of Western scholars studied Islam and Islamic civilizations, though often from a basis that has been considered "Orientalist," that is, expressing Western biases.

This rough outline of Christian-Muslim relations omits more than it says about the turbulent, usually conflictual relationship between Muslims and Christians. But Muslim Spain is often considered an exception to the low standard and is cited as representing the zenith of inter-religious harmony. Under Muslim rule, Christians and Jews in Spain were able to escape the oppressive feudal system that existed in the rest of Europe and to become prosperous, independent landowners. They served in the caliph's court as engineers, doctors, architects, and advisors.

Both Islamic and Jewish culture flourished, the two of them often intertwined. Spain became one of the main centers of Islamic scholarship and played a role in preserving the classical texts lost to Christian Europe during the early Middle Ages. These ancient Greek and Roman texts were eventually translated from Arabic into Latin and became the intellectual cornerstone of the European Renaissance.

In addition to preserving the scholarship of ancient Greece and Rome, Islamic architects, scholars, and scientists in Spain and elsewhere made their own contributions in architecture, mathematics, medicine, and physics. Few of us give much thought to the Arabic numerals we use every day in our daily lives, but the counting system popularized by the ninth-century mathematician Muhammad ibn Musa al-Khwarizmi, who is credited with inventing algebra, had an enormous impact on trade and finance when it was eventually adopted in Christian Europe several hundred years later. Hebrew prophecy and revelation and Greek philosophy and reasoning are considered the twin foundations of Western civilization; these also formed the foundations of Islamic civilization.

If Muslim Spain marked a high point in medieval tolerance, the Crusades marked a low. They were not directed specifically against Islam, the specific beliefs of which remained little known to Christians, but against an alien power that held Christianity's holy places (Speight, *God Is One*, pp. 89–90). The excesses and atrocities committed by Christian forces during the various Crusades created historical grievances that have lasted to this day among both Muslims and Orthodox Christians, who were often slaughtered alongside them. The cross became a symbol to Muslims not of Christian sacrifice and faith but of Western/ Christian aggression.

Following the Crusades, Christian and Muslim polemic increased, with both more willing to attribute error to the other religion. Christians variously depicted Islam as a heresy, a false religion, and even a diabolical force, with Muhammad portrayed as an epileptic, an unbeliever, and a sexual profligate. These negative stereotypes have persisted until the present and are echoed in the language of some contemporary political and religious leaders.

The Spanish Inquisition, instituted by the Catholic Church after the Christian reconquest of Spain, marked another period of increased conflict. Jews and Muslims were forced to convert to Christianity or face expulsion from Spain or even death. Like Muslims, many Jews sought sanctuary in North Africa and the Ottoman Empire, where as *dhimmis* (a protected minority) they and other People of the Book were allowed to practice their faith.

Christian-Muslim relations became further complicated by the advent of Western colonialism in the eighteenth century. Colonialism was often accompanied by intensive missionary activity in Muslim lands, and spreading Christianity served as justification for colonial rule. Western leaders sometimes attributed their success in taking over Muslim countries not only to their superior economic power and technology but to their superior religion and civilization. Muslims saw Christian missionary activity as supporting Western political rule, which increased their suspicion of Christianity.

Since World War II there have been some steps forward in Christian-Muslim relations. Three men in particular have played a prominent role in fostering Christian-Muslim understanding: the French diplomat and scholar Louis Massignon, for whom Islam played a key role in his return to the Catholic faith; the Anglican bishop Kenneth Cragg; and Wilfred Cantwell Smith of the United Church of Canada. All three were influential scholars whose work broke down barriers between Christians and Muslims.

A turning point in the Catholic Church's attitude toward both Islam and Judaism occurred during the Second Vatican Council with the promulgation in 1965 of *Nostra Aetate* (Declaration on the Relation of the Church with Non-Christian Religions), a document recognizing Muslims as a faith community to be respected, and affirming the need for Christians and Muslims to strive for mutual understanding. *Nostra Aetate* signaled even more important progress in the relations between Jews and Christians.

Since then the Catholic Church has taken further steps to develop interfaith understanding with both Muslims and Jews.

The attacks on the World Trade Center and the Pentagon on September 11, 2001, and the US-led invasions of Afghanistan and Iraq that followed have led to an upsurge in intercultural and inter-religious tension. Westerners, most of whom are Christians, tend to stereotype Muslims as religious fanatics filled with irrational hatred against the West. Muslims have just the opposite view. They regard the confrontation as one between Muslim faith and Western greed, between a Muslim way of life that encourages balance and moderation and a Western ethos encouraging violence and anarchy. Americans fear acts of terrorism; Muslims in developing countries fear that their societies could be obliterated in the blink of an eye by the much more powerful West. Alarm and suspicion have escalated on all sides of the religious divide.

MUSLIM-JEWISH RELATIONS

Like Christianity, Islam draws heavily on the Jewish Scriptures. The Quran is filled with references to the prophets of the Hebrew Scriptures and retells some of the same stories found there, though often elliptically, from another angle or with a different conclusion. Both Jewish and Christian tribes lived in Arabia during Muhammad's time, and his interactions with them are reflected in the Quran, which is alternately complimentary and critical of Christians and Jews. Non-Muslims often see the variance in tone as reflecting an evolution in Muhammad's thinking. As Muhammad realized that his revelations would not be universally accepted by Jews and Christians, he became more antagonistic toward them.

Concerning the Quran's treatment of Christians, Muslims tend to explain the variance by saying that the Quran describes two distinct Christian groups: a small band of faithful Christians who, like some Jews, are true believers in God, and a larger number who follow a distorted or corrupted version of Christianity (Peters, *Islam: A Guide for Jews and Christians*, p. 29). The

Quran portrays an even deeper ambivalence when it comes to Jews. The historical context for its critical remarks about Jews is the conflict between Muhammad and the Jews of Medina.

When Muhammad moved to Medina, the oasis, riven by political divisions, was looking for a charismatic leader and holy man who could resolve the differences that were tearing the city asunder. Muhammad reached out to the Jewish inhabitants of Medina, but many of them had ties to his opponents in Mecca and allied themselves with those Meccans as well as with other Medinans who opposed Muhammad's leadership.

The Quran reflects Muhammad's disappointment and growing combativeness as Jewish opposition to him persisted. The language became more truculent as the revelations continued in Medina and certain customs derived from Judaism changed. Initially, Muhammad had instructed his followers to pray facing Jerusalem, as Jews did, but sometime after he moved to Medina, the direction was changed to Mecca. The fast on Yom Kippur was also dropped. Instead, Muslims were to fast during Ramadan, the month in which Muhammad had received his first revelations from God.

Although there would be Jews in other places who welcomed the new revelation and became Muslims, the opposition from some of Medina's Jews led to their being driven from the city or killed. The Jews are portrayed in the Quran as God's chosen people, but also stubborn, faction-ridden, and contentious. The Quran speaks of a people who consistently turned away from God and refused to recognize Muhammad's authority.

Despite this fractious early history that is reflected in the Quran, Jews coexisted with Muslims in the emerging Muslim empire. When Jews were expelled from medieval Europe, they frequently sought and found refuge in Muslim societies. Because they were not allowed to proselytize or publicly worship, the protected "dhimmi" status granted People of the Book in the Ottoman Empire would be regarded as second-class citizenship today, yet for centuries Jews were given far more freedom and rights under the empire than they found in Christian Europe.

Jewish-Muslim relations took a turn for the worse with the rise of Zionism in the early twentieth century. Jewish nationalism and the search for a national home for the Jewish people took on added urgency because of the Jewish Holocaust during World War II and culminated in the founding of the state of Israel in 1948, and with it the displacement of much of the local Arab Palestinian population. Though the United Nations vote establishing Israel in 1948 partitioned Palestine with the intention of creating two states, the second Palestinian state has never been established. Because of Israeli opposition, United Nations resolutions calling for the repatriation or compensation of refugees have never been implemented. The situation of the Palestinian people remains unresolved to this day and is a continuing source of instability in the region.

Initially, the Arab-Israeli dispute was a political conflict rather than a religious one, but because Jerusalem is Islam's third most important holy site—the place where the archangel Gabriel conducted Muhammad on his Night Journey to Heaven—Israel's conquest of Jerusalem during the Six-Day War in 1967 made it of wider concern to Muslims. The humiliating defeat of the Arab countries involved came to be seen as symptomatic of a widespread malaise affecting Muslim societies in the Middle East.

Since then, Israel's occupation of the Palestinian territories it seized in the 1967 war has seeded increasing resentment among Muslims worldwide. They see the continuing occupation of the West Bank and Israel's control over Gaza as an injustice and a constant reminder of the humiliation that Western colonial powers have inflicted on Muslim societies. Because the United States is the primary sponsor of Israel, giving Israel several billion dollars a year in foreign aid and using its veto in the UN Security Council to shield Israel from negative diplomatic consequences that would otherwise accrue from its actions, Muslim hostility to the United States has grown alongside hostility to Israel. While support for Israel is not the only grievance the Muslim world has against the United States, it is an important one. Some Muslims think the United States uses Israel to sustain its own hegemony in the Middle East. They point to the posting of United States military forces in the Persian Gulf and United States support for undemocratic and repressive Middle Eastern governments that oppress their own populations as proof that the United States is interested in pursuing only its own interests at the cost of the people of the region.

CURRENT TENSIONS AND THEIR CAUSES

Religious Fundamentalism

The past thirty years have seen an upsurge in religious fundamentalism around the world, not only in Judaism, Islam, and Christianity but in other religions as well. Fundamentalism can be described as a militantly anti-modern school of thought that is itself a byproduct of modernity. The word "fundamentalism" was first coined to describe the views of some American Protestant Christians in the early part of the twentieth century who printed a series of pamphlets called "The Fundamentals" and who believed in biblical literalism and biblical prophecy. These fundamentalists took a gloomy view of the changes taking place in American society and in the 1920s withdrew from active participation in the larger society to their own religious enclaves. Beginning in the 1970s that changed, and fundamentalist Christians assumed an increasingly active and influential role in the political process.

Because it is a term taken from an American Christian experience, "fundamentalism" is not the preferred term to describe analogous movements in Judaism and Islam. For the latter, "Islamism" or "Islamic revivalism" is preferred. Nonetheless, the term "fundamentalism" is widely, if imprecisely, used to describe a parallel upsurge in an aggressive, back-to-basics religiosity among Christians, Jews, and Muslims, which, while extolling the original foundations of faith, often ignores or negates significant elements of the tradition as it has developed.

While fundamentalists can be particularly disparaging of members of their own faith community whom they see as betraying the principles of their faith by accepting or condoning the premises and practices of the modern world, they also sometimes adopt unapologetically antagonistic attitudes toward other religions. Fundamentalists believe that they are under siege by an increasingly secular and pluralistic culture. Their mission is to restore a sense of the sacred to the modern world. Though often criticized as anachronistic and primitive, fundamentalists tend to be innovators who appear only when the process of modernization is already well advanced. Not surprisingly, Muslim fundamentalism appeared on the scene later than Christian or Jewish fundamentalism, emerging during the 1960s and 1970s, when modernity began to take firm root in Muslim societies (Armstrong, *Islam*, p. 165).

In the United States the social turmoil of the 1960s spurred Christian fundamentalists to organize in an effort to reverse what they saw as dangerous secularizing trends that undermined the moral and religious basis of society. The 1960s also triggered a rise in Jewish and Muslim fundamentalism, though not for the same reasons. In different ways, the 1967 Arab-Israeli war was a turning point for many Israeli Jews and Arab Muslims as regards both their political fortunes and their religious and national identity. For Arabs, the crushing defeat that Israel inflicted on Egypt, Syria, and Jordan spelled an end to pan-Arabism, the latest "ism" that Arab countries had taken up in an effort to improve their political and economic fortunes. After decades of experimenting with monarchism, Western capitalism, secular nationalism, Marxist socialism, and pan-Arabism, with little discernible improvement in people's standard of living, many Muslims began turning to Islam as offering an indigenous, more authentic solution to the problems of their societies.

The last forty years have seen a general revival of religion in the Muslim world. For some Muslims, this has chiefly meant greater religious observance and attention to prayer, fasting, dress, and Islamic law or mysticism. For others, political Islam has become an inspiration and ideology. Like Christian fundamentalists who seek to influence the American political system to reflect their values, these politically oriented Islamists seek to reshape their societies through the application of Islamic principles to modern society. Islamists run the gamut from social reformers who have established clinics, schools, and social welfare organizations to help the poor, to those pressing for honest government and change via peaceful participation in the political process, to extremists who believe that violence is necessary to achieve their goals.

Islamists have often suffered persecution at the hands of the ruling elites, whose entrenched power and privilege they threaten. In most of the Muslim countries in which they live, Islamists have been discriminated against, jailed, or worse. The record indicates that when moderate Islamists are suppressed or marginalized by the state, more extremist Islamists often come to the fore. A cycle of violence begins in which harsh measures by the government trigger violent reactions by individuals and groups, which in turn provoke greater repression by the state, and so on.

For Israeli Jews, the Six-Day War was a tremendous victory that stimulated pride, nationalism, and even a sense of religious redemption. It also put them in possession of the whole historic area of Palestine. The line between God and country, religion and state, which was never clear-cut to begin with in a state defined by religion, grew more blurred. Israel became the nexus for a host of issues that concern all three faiths.

ISRAEL

Before and after the Roman Conquest and the destruction of the Second Temple in 70 c.e., the Jews were scattered. Though some still lived in the area known as Palestine, the great majority of them were dispersed around the globe. But even in the Diaspora, the land of Israel occupied a central place in Jewish history and faith. The phrase "Next year in Jerusalem" was repeated at the annual Passover celebration.

It was a staple of Jewish faith that eventually the Messiah would come at the end of time to usher in peace and prosperity. However, Jews were enjoined by their religious leaders not to seek to hasten the end of the world and even to treat messianic reports with a certain reserve. Yohanan ben Zakkai, a rabbi during the first-century Roman siege of Jerusalem, when Herod's Temple was destroyed, is reported to have said, "If you have a sapling in your hand and they say to you, 'The messiah has come,' finish planting the sapling and then receive him" (Gorenberg, *The End of Days*, p. 69).

Thus, early on, Zionism faced opposition from religious Jews who believed that it violated the injunction that Jews must do nothing to precipitate the arrival of the Messiah. Even today most ultra-Orthodox Jews do not serve in the Israeli military, and initially many Orthodox Jews did not recognize the state of Israel.

Zionism began in the late nineteenth century as a movement by secular Jews in Europe to create an alternative to the Jews' situation as a discriminated minority. Anti-Semitism was widespread in Christian Europe; Zionists believed that only when Jews had a state of their own could they become a people like any other people and be treated accordingly.

The early Zionists considered several places where they might establish a Jewish state, including Uganda and Argentina. For historical reasons, they decided on Palestine. From the turn of the twentieth century on, Jews began immigrating to Palestine as part of the Zionist project to form a Jewish state. Over time they met with opposition from the indigenous inhabitants, who viewed the Jewish newcomers as colonialists threatening their land and their livelihood and their own hopes for nationhood.

The Arabs in the region wanted independence from the Turkish Ottoman Empire and later from Great Britain, which administered Palestine as a Mandated Territory after the defeat of the Ottoman Empire in the First World War. In 1917 the British government issued the Balfour Declaration, which assured prominent Jews of Britain's support for the Zionist project; around the same time the British government also assured the Arabs support for their own nationalist aspirations. These irreconcilable promises set the stage for the conflict that was to come. Starting at the end of the 1920s, the struggle between Jews and

Palestinian Arabs for control of Palestine turned violent. In one form or another, the struggle has continued to this day, though the Zionists have been the clear and overwhelming winners.

The Six-Day War in 1967, in which Israel defeated its neighbors and gained control over all the original Mandate of Palestine, exacerbated friction between Jews and Muslims in the Mideast. Israel became an occupying power exercising control not only over additional territory but also over millions of Palestinians, including some who had fled the initial Arab-Israeli war in 1948. The harsh conditions that Israel imposed on the Palestinians under occupation led to further Muslim resentment as they saw the world ignoring Israel's violations of international law and human rights. Christian Palestinians were subjected to the same conditions as Muslim Palestinians, but with greater resources and connections to the West, many responded by emigrating from the Holy Land; they are now a small percentage of the Palestinian population living in the West Bank and Gaza.

If the Six-Day War gave Muslims a greater stake in the conflict, it also stimulated the attention and interest of Jews both inside and outside Israel and of many Christians living in the United States. The Israeli conquest of Palestine fed both Jewish pride and Jewish religious messianism. In violation of international law but abetted by the state of Israel, Zionist religious Jews (including many who had come to Israel from the United States) began settling the new territories, which they believed to be a religious duty that would lead to divine redemption and the coming of the long-awaited Messiah.

For their part, many fundamentalist Christians saw Israel's victory as a milestone confirming their understanding of how the creation of Israel in 1948 figured in biblical prophecy. In their literalist reading of the Bible, Israel is important because without it there can be no Rapture, no Armageddon leading to the end times. While this is not standard Christian theology (the Catholic Church and most mainline Protestant churches dissent from a literalist reading of the Bible and see the focus on the actual political state of Israel as a distortion of traditional

Christian theology), fundamentalist Christians have organized themselves into a potent political force. They have become strong supporters of the state of Israel, to the point of opposing peace negotiations with the Palestinians. Together with American Jews, a strong and politically influential lobby, they have worked to maintain the United States' unstinting military, economic, and diplomatic support for Israel and its occupation of Palestinian lands.

American Jews are not apt to share fundamentalist Christians' emphasis on biblical prophecy, particularly as it foretells the destruction of all those who are not true Christians, but the memory of the Jewish Holocaust has given many American Jews a strong commitment to Israel as a Jewish state that offers a safe haven to Jews around the world. For some, the historical injustices committed against Jews in the past and the need to assure Jewish security are so great as to negate any claims Palestinians might themselves have to justice and security. For others, the state of Israel has become integral to Jewish identity. To a surprising degree, Zionism, once a secular socialist political project opposed by Jewish orthodoxy, has become firmly entrenched as an essential element of Judaism, as much in the United States as in Israel.

Unfortunately, the passage of time has not made the Israeli-Palestinian issue any less intractable. If anything, it has only furthered resentments and fanned the flames of inter-religious hostility. Muslims in the Middle East, particularly Palestinian Arabs, feel bitter that they have had to pay the price for European anti-Semitism by surrendering land for a Jewish state at the dictates of Western colonial powers, which gave away land that was not theirs to give. Haunted by the genocide of World War II, Israeli Jews have been determined not to offer any advantage to their Palestinian adversaries, including fundamental political and economic rights. As the conflict has dragged on, anti-Semitism, a product of Christian Europe, has begun to filter into the discourse of the Muslim population of the Middle East. Meanwhile anti-Arab and anti-Muslim sentiment, long present in Israel, has grown stronger in the West with the immigration of many Muslims to Europe.

Because of the upsurge in fundamentalism, the religious element in the quarrel between Israeli Jews and Palestinian Arabs over land and resources has grown rather than diminished with the passage of time. Jewish religious settlers on the West Bank attempt to drive Palestinian Arabs from a land Arabs have lived on for centuries in the belief that God has promised the land to the Jews and to Jews alone, while Islamist groups such as Hamas and Islamic Jihad sometimes link their opposition to Israel not only to Israel's confiscation of Palestinian land but to the Quran's criticisms of Jewish tribes in Medina. Even the Palestinian Authority, which has always been a secular nationalist entity, has begun to speak more in Islamist terms. The 2006 election of Hamas in the Palestinian territories is a further sign of how a political struggle is taking on increased religious coloration.

Jerusalem, where all three Abrahamic religions have holy sites, is a particular flashpoint. The stunning shrine of the Dome of the Rock is the place from which tradition has it that Muhammad, riding his celestial steed Buraq, ascended to the Heavenly House of Life in the seventh heaven. There, within two bow-shots of God's presence, he conversed with God and persuaded God to reduce his demand that Muslims pray fifty times a day to five.

The Dome of the Rock, along with the al-Aqsa mosque, is situated in an area that Muslims call the Noble Sanctuary and Jews call the Temple Mount. This lies a stone's throw from the Wailing Wall and over the remains of what is believed to be Solomon's Temple, Judaism's holiest place. A small minority of extremist religious Jews, as well as some extreme Christian fundamentalists, want to destroy the Dome of the Rock in order to rebuild the Temple. Several plots to destroy the mosque have been discovered and, fortunately, averted. But such plots, if carried through, could set off a religious explosion that could convulse the entire region. Not only is the Dome of the Rock a holy shrine, but, like other religious sites in Israel and the occupied territories, it has become a nationalist symbol as well, and for that reason all the more potent.

While religion is a relatively minor factor in the Israeli-Palestinian struggle, cynical elements have sometimes had an interest in exaggerating its importance, either to exploit religious emotions or to discredit the other side's legitimate political grievances. Some sympathizers with Israel like to present the Israeli-Palestinian conflict as one driven by Muslim hatred of Jews, preferring to ignore the Christian identity of some Palestinians and Israel's ongoing occupation and expropriation of Palestinian territory in favor of an emotionally charged explanation that will omit any Israeli accountability for the hostilities. Similarly, some Muslims may charge a Western conspiracy against Muslim societies because this is a way to capture other Muslims' attention and command their loyalty. The idea that the Israeli-Palestinian struggle is an age-old religious conflict that goes back centuries is inaccurate. Rather, a political dispute over land and resources that emerged in the twentieth century has exploited and encouraged religious chauvinism.

THE NEED FOR DIALOGUE

While the Israeli-Palestinian conflict may be the most inflammatory interreligious conflict today, there are others. Muslims and Hindus are in conflict over Kashmir; Christians and Muslims have clashed in Sudan, Pakistan, Nigeria, and the Philippines. In most of these countries, religious hostility or rivalry is but one element in a complex mix of issues that are usually rooted in specific political and economic grievances that sometimes have little per se to do with religion. Frequently these complexities tend to be reduced to simplistic religious stereotypes that fan religious animosities and ignore more fundamental issues.

An additional source of tension is created by the presence of large Muslim minorities in many countries. About a quarter of all Muslims live as a religious minority population. Akbar S. Ahmed, professor at Cambridge University, points out that no other religion in the world has so many of its adherents living in an alien environment (Ahmed, *Islam Today*, p. 165).

In the United States the previously small Muslim population has grown rapidly during the last thirty-five years. A large proportion of Muslims in the United States and Canada are middle-class doctors, engineers, and academics with a sophisticated, worldly perspective. In Europe, however, sizeable and frequently impoverished immigrant communities exist that are not assimilated into the society.

European governments initially encouraged immigration because of the cheap labor Muslim immigrants provided or because of a colonial relationship in which the inhabitants of former colonies were allowed to immigrate to the European home country. While some immigrants have certainly prospered in Europe, others live on the fringes of society as a marginalized underclass. The strain on the social fabric is evident in the rise of racist, anti-immigrant sentiment among those who consider themselves native Europeans and in a dangerous alienation from the majority culture on the part of young, often unemployed or underemployed Muslim youth, who feel like second-class citizens.

Hateful rhetoric is on the rise, amplified by the media, which often focuses on extremist statements and behavior as if they were typical rather than exceptions. In many Muslim countries, rabid anti-Christian and anti-Semitic literature is widely available. The Protocols of Zion, an anti-Semitic literary hoax discredited long ago, circulates unchallenged.

Among both Muslims and Westerners, polarizing or extremist statements demonizing other people's culture or religious faith are increasingly common. Nowadays one sometimes hears that Muslims hate Christians and Jews. As a description of the beliefs of hundreds of millions of persons, this is at best a gross distortion. It ignores the respect paid to Jews and Christians in the Quran, which is reflected in popular practice in the custom of choosing biblical names for Muslim children, as in Issa (Jesus), Musa (Moses), Sulayman (Solomon), and Ibrahim (Abraham). Whenever Muslims mention these and other biblical prophets, they add the words "Peace be upon him" as a sign of reverence, just as they do when mentioning Muhammad.

Universalism has historically been part of the Muslim tradition. According to the Quran, all People of the Book share in the hope of eternal salvation: "Verily, they who believe (Muslims), and they who follow the Jewish religion, and the Christians, and the Sabeites—whoever of these believeth in God and the last day, and doth that which is right, shall have their reward with their Lord: fear shall not come upon them, neither shall they be grieved" (Sura 2:59).

Elsewhere the Quran urges peace between the different faith communities: "Say: In whatsoever Books God hath sent down do I believe: I am commanded to decide justly between you: God is your Lord and our Lord: we have our works and you have your works: between us and you let there be no strife: God will make us all one: and to Him shall we return" (Sura 42:13).

The religious animadversions common these days stem largely from ignorance and historical prejudice. They underscore the need for dialogue between different peoples and faiths. Learning more about other people's religion and culture will not necessarily produce agreement on all issues, but it will curtail some of the myths that are based in ignorance or inaccurate information. The United States' own small but growing Muslim population makes it all the more important that Americans become better informed about Islam.

MUSLIMS IN THE UNITED STATES

Most Americans are largely unaware of the fact that the Muslim presence in the United States goes back to before the nineteenth century. Some of the early explorers, traders, and settlers in North America were Muslims, and an estimated 15 percent of the slaves brought to the United States from the sixteenth to the nineteenth century were Muslims. While Muslim slaves were not allowed to keep their religion, other Muslims who came to North America did.

The Muslim population was tiny, however; the first significant Muslim immigration took place during the late nineteenth century when Middle Easterners, most of them from the region of Syria, arrived in the United States to take blue-collar jobs. A second wave of better-educated Muslims immigrants, drawn from not only the Middle East but also the Soviet Union and Eastern Europe, followed after World War I. The liberalized immigration law of 1965 set the stage for a third and larger wave of well-educated immigrants, most of them professionals, which has increased the Muslim population exponentially. Today it is estimated that six to eight million Muslims live in the United States. They include Muslim immigrants from over eighty countries, making the United States Muslim population one of the most ethnically diverse Muslim populations in the world. Nowhere outside of Mecca during the hajj can one see such a rich representation of different Muslim cultures.

About 20 to 25 percent of the Muslims living in the United States are African American converts to Islam. Spurred by pan-African ideas, African Americans began taking an interest in Islam in the early decades of the twentieth century as a way to reconnect to their African roots. A number of new African American religions were established, including, in 1930, the Nation of Islam. This religion appealed specifically to black nationalism and preached the gospel of black self-reliance, education, and community self-defense.

In its early years the Nation of Islam had little in common with Islam other than the name. Its most famous follower was Malcolm X, who became a minister in the Nation of Islam and the public face of black militancy during a tumultuous era in which American blacks struggled to gain their civil rights. After making the hajj in 1963, Malcolm X was so moved by his experience at Mecca that he broke with the Nation of Islam and embraced normative Islam. He was murdered by two members of the Nation of Islam two years later. His memoir, *The Autobiography of Malcolm X*, was enormously influential. Partly because of it, in the 1960s and 1970s many American blacks turned to Islam, which was seen as an alternative to a Christianity that had conspired in their oppression. In time, after the death of its founder in 1975, the Nation of Islam also moved to embrace mainstream Islam, abandoning the black supremacism that had earlier characterized it under the leadership of Elijah Muhammad. After the dissolution of the Nation of Islam, Minister Louis Farrakhan formed a reconstituted organization that retains many of the movement's original ideas.

Islam continues to draw many African American converts, particularly in United States prisons, where its message of social justice and its moral discipline have been an inspiration and aid to many prisoners to reform their lives. But Islam is increasingly appealing to white and Hispanic Americans as well. While immigration and a high birth rate are the first two factors that account for the growing Muslim population in the United States, conversion is the third, and recent studies indicate that Islam can no longer be considered a protest religion of interest only to African Americans. Many expect that in the twenty-first century, Islam will become the second largest religion after Christianity in the United States.

Muslims in the United States face the challenge of practicing their faith in an environment that is not always hospitable to them. The secular American workplace is typically not receptive to Muslim employees breaking off their duties to pray; finding *halal* (permitted) food can be difficult; upholding religious teachings and traditional social mores and customs can be difficult in the more permissive United States environment. Indeed, it is estimated that only about a fourth of the Muslims in the United States practice their faith.

Muslims in the United States are also challenged to create a viable community from a disparate population drawn from many different backgrounds and cultures and holding many different points of view. If the first waves of Muslim immigrants assimilated quickly into American culture, often to the point of losing touch with Muslim teachings and traditions, the last, larger wave brought many Muslims to the United States who were uninterested in assimilation; they shared many of the attitudes and objectives common to the worldwide revival of Islam, including an insistence on head coverings for women, halal foods, and a preference for retaining their own ethnic and religious traditions.

But the biggest test confronting Muslims living in the United States today is the post-9/11 environment. Following the attacks of September 11, 2001, thousands of Muslims were deported; millions of dollars in bank accounts for Muslim causes and charities were frozen; prominent Muslim leaders were arrested and charged with terrorism, though these charges were often later reduced to minor violations. In addition to enduring intense scrutiny, and in some cases harassment, by government agencies, Muslims found themselves the object of public mistrust. Public opinion polls show that many Americans hold negative and prejudicial ideas about Islam, with one poll conducted by the Council on American-Islamic Relations (CAIR) indicating that roughly 25 percent of the American public think that Islam teaches hatred and violence. Unfortunately, this emerging "Islamophobia" has been encouraged by some Christian leaders, over-zealous supporters of Israel, conservative talk-show hosts, and so-called "experts" who paint Islamic centers as terrorist havens promoting jihadist indoctrination.

In self-defense, American Muslims are making more vigorous efforts to explain their faith to an often-skeptical public. They are participating in interfaith dialogues, interacting in the public square, and organizing at the grassroots level. This is a time of both new opportunities and new dangers for Muslims in the United States, who are often frustrated by the public expectations of them. They are constantly asked to prove their American loyalty and condemn violence, but however often they do so, their condemnations frequently go unreported, unheard, and ignored. The actions of a few individuals at home and abroad draw enormous attention and place the entire Muslim population under a cloud of suspicion that individuals cannot easily dispel. Those familiar with American history know that many other ethnic and religious groups—Catholics, Jews, Irish Americans, German Americans, Japanese Americans, and others—have faced similar periods of mistrust and discrimination.

THE PROMISE OF DIALOGUE

Greater knowledge about Muslims' faith and situation may enhance understanding of the sources of, and solutions to, conflicts between Muslims and Western nations. But inter-religious dialogue has other benefits as well. At its best, it carries with it the potential to revivify and refresh the religious perspective of all those involved. Christians and Jews who become familiar with Islam will find much in it to respect and admire, much that can invigorate their own approach to religious belief and practice. Louis Massignon, the great French scholar of Islam whose study led him to both revere and cherish Islam and to rediscover his own Christian faith, wrote that Judaism is a religion of hope, Christianity a religion of love, and Islam a religion of faith.

Insofar as hope, love, and faith are all part of a relationship with God and with our fellow human beings, a greater acquaintance with all three religions can serve those who study them.

CHAPTER 5

Islam Today

If American Christians were asked to assess the state of Christianity today, they would most likely look to their own country first. There they would see a large and diverse population of believers confronted with many issues on which there is no general consensus. Not only do American Christians hold different views about Christian faith and doctrine—hence the many denominations in the United States—but they also disagree about political, social, and economic issues facing their country.

There are Christian conservatives who would like to see their brand of conservative Christianity reflected much more in American culture. They agitate for prayer in school and the teaching of intelligent design; they oppose abortion, same-sex marriage, and embryonic stem cell research, and are concerned about a moral decline in society.

There are Christian liberals who support abortion rights, same-sex marriage, and embryonic stem cell research but oppose the death penalty and would like the government to reduce military spending in favor of social programs to benefit the disadvantaged and do more to curb pollution and global warming.

Both of these groups see Christianity as a motive force in their lives, but their views have brought them to very different political positions. Other Christians fall somewhere in the political middle, or are either apolitical or have so compartmentalized

89

their faith that they are disinclined to draw connections between religion and politics.

If United States Christians cast their gaze further afield, beyond their own society, they would see an even greater diversity in Christian belief and practice. In addition to Catholics and Protestants, the spectrum widens to include the various Orthodox churches around the world and the many Christians living in developing countries in Asia, Africa, and Latin America. Christianity is growing most rapidly in the Third World, and here, in more traditional societies, Christians lead lives that are very different from those of Christians living in the United States and Europe. Not surprisingly, their concerns are often different, too.

Compared with Christianity with its two billion adherents, Judaism, with fourteen to eighteen million adherents, has a much smaller population confined to a more geographically restricted area. But Jews, too, are an internally diverse community, with secular Jews having few apparent commonalities with ultra-Orthodox Jews, who wear distinctive eighteenth-century clothing, keep strict dietary laws, eschew modern conveniences to observe the Sabbath, and spend much of their time in prayer and study.

Islam also presents a study in contrasts. Muslims around the world are a large and heterogeneous population of 1.2 billion people. While a remarkable uniformity of practice unites Muslims, nationality and ethnicity shape their customs and concerns, just as they do Christians and Jews. Indonesian Muslims, Turkish Muslims, Iranian Muslims, Arab Muslims, Pakistani and Indian Muslims, Muslims in China, Muslims in Chechnya and the many nations in Africa and Europe inhabit distinct and different cultures that color their attitudes toward life, politics, and religion.

These differences in culture, nationality, race, and ethnicity are the most striking signs of the diversity that Islam comprises, but hardly the only ones. There are many different interpretations of the Quran and the sunna, many legal and social differences, and many schools of theology and philosophy that have contributed to the rich intellectual tradition of Islam.

Despite this cultural and intellectual diversity, Islam has preserved its cohesiveness even in the midst of multiple traditions. In Islam, as in Christianity, the inner attitude determines whether one is a Muslim or a Christian, yet Muslims are challenged to express their faith through action, through the ethical transformation of their societies. From the time of the first umma that Muhammad established, politics has been integrally tied to Islamic spirituality, law, and philosophy. A Muslim demonstrates his faith in reverence and obedience to God, in complete surrender to God's will, and in the honesty, compassion, magnanimity, and hospitality he or she exhibits toward others. Called to be both God's perfect servants and his vice-regents on earth, Muslims see the implementation of a just society as intrinsic to their duty to redeem the world. Notwithstanding the fact that Muslims have rarely lived in societies that lived up to the Quranic vision, that vision continues to shape the ideals and expectations Muslims live by.

Of course, the unity that has always been so emphasized in Islam does not mean uniformity. With more than a billion Muslims in the world, there are Muslims with every conceivable point of view: secular Muslims, conservative Muslims, liberal Muslims, "fundamentalist" Muslims. Even those labels can be misleading. Some of those characterized as "fundamentalist" urge returning to the form of Islam practiced during the time of Muhammad and advocate a state run according to Islamic law; others are religious Muslims who lead pious lives and do not concern themselves with politics.

Other terms employed to describe Muslim belief can be equally slippery: revivalist, reformist, liberal, traditionalist, progressive, modernist. Indeed, the resurgence of Islam in the last forty years, the reassertion of religious identity and practice in both private and public life, has been variously called Islamic renewal, Islamic revivalism, Islamism, and Islamic fundamentalism. These terms can and do mean something slightly different to specialists, but in popular usage they are often employed interchangeably. At the heart of Muslim renewal, however, is the belief that Muslim societies are in decline and that only through a rededication to the principles of Islam and the implementation of religious law can Muslim societies hope for a restoration of Islamic values, identity, and power (Esposito, *The Islamic Threat*, p. 17).

Before discussing the spectrum of opinions held by Muslims today, it is important to see Islam in historical context as both a religion and a civilization. At its peak, the latter extended over half of the Eastern hemisphere, profoundly affecting Muslims and other peoples who lived within the complex of cultures that demarcated Islamic civilization, and influencing through its interaction with other civilizations the course of world history.

But "Islamdom" has been in decline for several centuries, eclipsed by the power of the West in the modern period. Despite frequent references to the Muslim world, it has been observed that there has not been a separate "Muslim world" for two hundred years. One scholar points out that there is no spontaneous Islamic movement after the European colonization of Muslim countries; that all such movements "are reacting to some force, or series of forces, that emanate from the Western world" (Lawrence, *Shattering the Myth*, p. 45) Colonization and globalization are, and have been for decades, the framework within which modern Islamic movements operate.

THE ROLE OF IMPERIALISM

Islam's rapid expansion after the death of Muhammad occurred under Muhammad's immediate successors as caliph and then under the Umayyad caliphate (661–750 c.e.), which was followed by the Abbasid caliphate. Abbasid rule lasted from the middle of the eighth century to the middle of the thirteenth. This period is often considered the golden age of Islam because of the flowering of Islamic arts, philosophy, and science. Eventually the power of the Abbasid caliphate began to wane. The caliph became a symbol of Islamic unity rather than a temporal ruler making essential on-the-ground decisions, and power in the Muslim world shifted to various local dynasties, the most significant of them Persian and Turkic. In the fourteenth century the Ottoman Turks founded a vast, long-lived empire that included Syria, North Africa, Arabia, and the Balkans. In the sixteenth century the Safavid Empire was established in Iran, and the Mughal Empire in India.

During this time Islamdom continued to expand, reaching its maximum extension in the seventeenth century. This was the time when Europe began making scientific, technological, and political gains. Soon European powers were pressing ahead militarily and putting pressure on the perimeters of Muslim lands. Like the expansion of Islam in the seventh and eighth centuries, this expansion had little to do with religion per se, yet its effect was to bring Muslim societies under European control. Eventually all Muslim societies fell under colonial rule, with the exception of Turkey, Saudi Arabia, Afghanistan, and Iran. Even these countries felt the effect of colonialism with Turkey, the central province of the Ottoman Empire, forced to make constant concessions to the Western powers during the long waning years of the Ottoman Empire.

The challenge that the West presented to Muslim societies as well as other pre-modern cultures was unprecedented in history. Never before had one civilization succeeded in dominating the world so entirely. Instead of being based on agriculture, Western economies relied on technology and capital investment, and in so doing escaped the inherent limitations of agrarian economies. The Industrial Revolution that followed in the West seemed to guarantee limitless progress with its technical innovations and the greater availability of mass-produced goods. In making efficiency the watchword of the new system, the West also put a premium on political and social values that would facilitate the new economic order. Thus democracy, tolerance, and secularism accompanied economic modernization as necessary concomitants to the new world order being created (Armstrong, *Islam*, p. 143).

Capitalism in the West demanded new markets in order to expand. Hence European countries began colonizing countries to draw them into its commercial network. The problem for the colonized countries was that a process that had evolved in the

West over three hundred years was abruptly, and indeed traumatically, forced on them. The hallmarks of modernization in Europe and the United States were innovation and autonomy. But agrarian countries elsewhere were forced into an essentially imitative role in trying to catch up to the West. And whereas Europe and the United States had experienced a growing political freedom during a long, tumultuous period marked by religious wars and revolutions and industrial expansion and exploitation, colonized countries experienced modernization as a loss of freedom and autonomy (Armstrong, *Islam*, p. 145). They were subjugated to foreign powers and forced to play catch-up against the modern West. Even when their economies made progress in modernizing, the pace of continuing innovations in the West meant that these societies gained little ground vis-à-vis the West. They seemed doomed to slip ever further behind.

Strategic locations in the Muslim world were the first to be subjected to colonization. Even before Napoleon's invasion of Egypt in 1798, the British had penetrated India and the Dutch East Indies. But the Napoleonic invasion and occupation of the heartland of Islamdom marked a decisive turn of fortune that Muslims found impossible to ignore or oppose. Following Napoleon's conquest of Egypt, one Muslim country after another was colonized and occupied. Ignoring the fact that their own societies' pre-modern past was not so very different, the Western colonizers frequently plumed themselves on what they regarded as their superiority to the backward, fatalistic natives they ruled over, who, not unnaturally, did not appreciate such condescension.

In time, nationalism, a phenomenon that originated in the West, began to exercise an influence on local Muslim populations, where it contributed to the formation of secular national liberation movements against Western imperialism. Arguably, nationalism has been the single most determining force in the Middle East, as in Europe, Africa, and Asia, during the twentieth century. Even the recent pan-Islamic movement often serves a nationalist agenda, one that has simply been recast in a more Islamic mold. Significantly, political Islam was launched not by religious figures but by intellectuals, who believed it could provide an effective alternative to nationalism, secular capitalism, and Marxist socialism, all of which had been tried and all of which had failed to help the mass of Muslims escape poverty and oppression. For proponents who believed that Islam could provide not just a religion but a total system of being, involving everything from law and justice to economics and foreign policy, political Islam appeared an indigenous and authentic answer to both colonialist domination and the need for social reform.

In the 1950s and 1960s, Egyptian president Gamal Abdel Nasser had ignited enthusiasm throughout the Arab world with his vision of pan-Arab nationalism and socialism, but his vision of Arab unity failed to overcome rivalry between Arab societies and rulers and proved diplomatically and militarily impotent, as shown by Israel's swift defeat of Arab countries in the 1967 Six-Day War. In the ensuing disillusionment, Islam as a political program took on currency as a possible solution to Muslim helplessness.

In drawing political direction from their faith, Muslims were not doing anything unique to Islam. The American civil rights movement began in United States churches, where people saw Christianity as a basis for challenging the injustice that relegated American blacks to second-class citizenship. In the 1970s conservative Christians entered the political arena, galvanized by the social changes of the 1960s. Still very much a force today, the religious right opposed what they saw as godless liberalism overturning the traditional foundations of morality and establishing new and dangerous social trends. Political Christianity, whether of the left or the right, has been a significant force in United States politics during the past half-century. Zionism, Jewish nationalism, has been even more successful. Political Zionism has provided both secular and religious Jews with a new and powerful source of Jewish identity. It may be that in the modern era individuals of whatever faith tradition find it easier to locate religious meaning in the political here and now than in traditional cultic practices. Historically, all religions seek to provide believers with a comprehensive way of life, not simply a privatized experience.

During the wave of anti-colonialism that followed World War II, one country after another in the Middle East and Africa gained its independence. Often the borders of these new nations had been determined by colonial powers with little regard for natural boundaries or economic or political viability. They frequently reflected Western interests more than the interests of the inhabitants, and the creation of these new political entities was modeled after the Western nation-state rather than more indigenous forms of political organization. Disparate ethnicities were brought together under a national banner but had little national allegiance or consciousness.

The Western-oriented elites that took over the reins of government in these newly independent states were usually closer in education and outlook to their previous colonial overlords than to the public they served. They identified modernization with Westernization and saw religion as an obstacle to be overcome. A process of Westernization and secularization was begun that entailed immense changes, yet the mass of people continued to hold traditional beliefs, even in those societies where modernization proceeded swiftly. Significantly, it is precisely in those countries where modernization has advanced most—Egypt, Lebanon, Iran—that Islamic resurgence has taken strongest root (Esposito, *The Islamic Threat*, p. 7–8).

Unfortunately, the post-colonial period has not met the high expectations people had on gaining independence. Despite modernization programs, many Muslim societies in the Middle East have not made economic and political progress. Instead, they have seen growing economic injustice and social inequality. Unemployment is high and the political culture often stultified; Western values, often the worst rather than the best of them, continue to dominate and, if anything, have become more powerful. In response, some Muslims perceive their societies as colonized twice—first politically and economically, and later culturally. The prevalence of American programs on TV and radio in developing countries means that people outside the United States are constantly exposed to American culture, and frequently the most materialistic, decadent, or sensationalistic aspects of it. People in more traditional societies can be fascinated, attracted, or repulsed by it or feel a combination of all three responses.

Especially in the Middle East, post-colonial governments have not presented any kind of decisive break with colonial administration but have perpetuated policies widely regarded as corrupt, undemocratic, and self-interested, directed more toward keeping the governing elites in power than helping elevate and advance all members of society. This in turn has spawned citizens' antagonism to their own government, and in many cases to the United States for backing it. In addition to being disliked for its support of autocratic, unpopular regimes, the United States is also resented for maintaining a neocolonialist military presence in the Persian Gulf and for pressuring Arab governments to comply with its foreign policy objectives.

Along with complaints about a United States double standard in the Israeli-Palestinian conflict, United Nations economic sanctions placed on Iraq after the first Gulf War, at the insistence of the United States, seemed to many Muslims (as well as many non-Muslims) draconian and unjust, especially once the sanctions' lethal effects on Iraqi children in particular became clear. Collective punishment was being imposed on an entire society, and it was the Iraqi people, not its leaders, who were suffering because of it. The silence of the United States as regards Russian atrocities in Chechnya, the slowness of the United States to react to the slaughter of Bosnian Muslims in the 1990s, and the failure of the United States to oppose the suppression of democracy in Algeria in 1992, when Algerian Islamists were fraudulently denied victory at the polls, appeared to many Muslims to underscore United States hypocrisy about human rights and democracy.

More recently, the 2003 United States-led invasion of Iraq has angered large numbers of Muslims, who perceive the United States as embarking on a new course of imperialist domination to wrest control of strategic resources like oil for its own citizens. Perceptions of the United States as unjust, bullying, and hypocritical are held by a wide range of Muslims. They form an important part of the backdrop to the current tensions between Muslims and the West.

POLITICS AND GOVERNMENT

The vast majority of Muslims today live in undemocratic states ruled by governments that rely on police and security forces to stay in power and that keep careful watch over their population. Most of these states are secular and modernizing, and several are openly hostile to religion (China, Turkey, and many of the new Central Asian countries that were part of the former Soviet Union). A few are Islamic states (the monarchy of Saudi Arabia and the Islamic Republic of Iran), but in very few are democratic freedoms permitted. Lacking in popular legitimacy, some of these states use religion to bolster their authority, though at other times, when it seems necessary or expedient, they will make religion an excuse to persecute their population. The threat of "Muslim extremism" becomes a rationale for suppressing those elements of the citizenry that challenge the government.

The monarchs, emirs, and military dictators who predominate in Muslim-majority countries decide how Islamic the state should be and present whatever version of Islam they decide on as normative. Most countries offer some kind of lip service to Islam but, as their citizens are well aware, are far from living up to the ideals of justice, fraternity, and egalitarianism expressed in the Quran. Accordingly, Islam serves as a reservoir of potential political dissent, as it has throughout Muslims' history. On the practical level, in the modern national security state the mosque is often one of the few places where people can freely meet and mingle. On a spiritual and political level, the faithful can argue that a government that deviates so seriously from what a just society should be does not deserve to stay in power. Both because the traditions of Islam favor this and because the political climate excludes other avenues for dissent, issues of political governance tend to be expressed in religious terms.

MUSLIM RESPONSES TO WESTERNIZATION

Over the years Muslims have reacted in different ways to Western dominance and the challenge it poses to their societies and their religion. Secularists have attributed Western pre-eminence to the outmoded traditions of Islam and have advocated a modern nation-state constructed along European lines that would separate state and religion. Conservatives, including most of the ulama, have blamed the decline of their societies on Muslims turning their back on God and the traditions of Islam, and have urged a rejection of Western values. Modernists and reformists responded to the crises of their society by seeking to reinterpret Islam and adapt it to modern life but possessed different perspectives on how to do so.

To explain further: Broadly speaking, the word "modernist" as applied to Islam refers to those Muslims who, beginning in the nineteenth century, saw the economic and technological backwardness of their societies and believed that Islam had to modernize by adopting the system of scientific and rational values that generate technology. The modernists saw Western culture as providing a model that Muslim societies should emulate if they hoped to prosper in the modern world. They advocated jettisoning those aspects of Islam that they did not see as rational or relevant and making Islam more adaptive to the modern world.

One prominent early modernist, Ahmad Khan (1817–1898), wanted to abandon the sunna, the traditions of what Muhammad said or did, which Khan considered unreliable, and spoke of "conformity to nature" as a criterion by which Islam and other religions should be judged. In any conflict between what religion teaches and what is taught by nature, known through reason and the senses, Khan said the teachings of religion should be thrown out. Modernist views held by Khan and others spurred social and educational reforms, prompted Muslims in many places to reject blind conformity to tradition, encouraged a reform of Sufi practices, and offered a vision of Islam that stressed its progressive, reasonable, and democratic character.

Many Muslim modernists were great admirers of the West, especially its science and technology. Anti-colonialists before independence, they were later frequently influenced by Marxism, existentialism, structuralism, and other Western philosophies. Modernism continues to guide the governments of most Muslim-majority states today, even though modernism as a political philosophy has been increasingly discredited in the eyes of many of their citizens.

"Reformist" or "neo-revivalist" are terms used to describe Muslims who embrace Western technology but not Western culture and who self-consciously assert their Muslim identity. Partly because they were able to appeal to conservative Muslims, who believed that the failure of Muslim societies to prosper was due to Muslims' turning away from religion, and partly because of their discipline, the reformists have been more influential than the modernists. The latter have been criticized for adopting Western values wholesale rather than developing a new synthesis of Islam and modernity.

The reformists, on the other hand, insist that all modernization needs to be rooted in Islamic values. The reformists call for Muslims to live according to the Quran and the sunna. They believe that by implementing Islamic law, they can create a more authentic Islamic society. Just as the early Protestants emphasized the Bible and wanted to purify the Catholic faith of what they saw as the agglutinations and corruptions that had developed over centuries, many Muslim reformists, like many modernists as well, have emphasized the early years of Islam at the expense of fourteen centuries of Islamic history, philosophy, and theology.

Critics assert that Muslim reformists want to return Islam to an idyllic past that in fact never existed. Indeed, some reformists have rejected not only Western secularism and materialism but the artistic and sacred artifacts of Islam in the name of a purer Islam that they proclaim. Whereas Muslim traditionalists are often characterized as wanting to preserve the best of the past, many reformists are described as wanting to revive the past.

While modernism and reformism form two Muslim responses to Westernization, there are other Muslim points of view that should be mentioned. Some modernists are also liberals, a point of view that stresses the subjectivity of truth and urges dialogue between those of different views. Muslim liberals locate in their religion support for freedom, democracy, and human rights and point to the Quran's strictures on consultation and community consensus as well as the hadith. (Muhammad is famously reported to have said, "My community will never agree on an error.")

Categorizing Muslims as liberals, reformists, modernists, or conservatives can be a convenient way to talk about some of the currents that affected Islam in the twentieth century and continue to do so today. However, the vast majority of Muslims would probably not recognize themselves in any of these categories. Like most Christians and Jews, most Muslims try to follow the dictates of their religion as best they can but are too busy with their lives to take up causes of one kind or another or to reflect at length on how their faith should develop. They pray, go to the mosque, fast during Ramadan, celebrate the holidays, and try to lead ethical lives. Still others have only a tenuous relationship to their faith. They are born into Muslim societies; their parents or grandparents may have been Muslim, but they do not observe the duties of Islam and may have only the haziest notion of what Islam teaches.

Just as the strength of traditional Christianity has faded in the West due to modernization, Islam has also been affected by modern values. Nonetheless, a far greater number of Muslims than Western Christians continue to practice their faith. The Muslim resurgence testifies to the relevance that Islam continues to hold for believers, as does the very fact that violence is committed in the name of the religion. For many centuries Western Christians also waged wars in the name of their religion before nationalism, fascism, communism, and other ideologies displaced Christianity as a more important source of Westerners' identity and allegiance.

ISLAMISM

An extreme form of reformism is Islamism, or Islamic fundamentalism. Notwithstanding Western stereotypes, most Islamic fundamentalists are not violent, bomb-throwing extremists. According to Lawrence Davidson, professor of history at West Chester University in Pennsylvania and author of the book *Islamic Fundamentalism*, the vast majority are "very much like your average very religious Catholic or Protestant" (*NCR*, Oct. 8, 2004).

Like Christian fundamentalists, many Islamists oppose certain aspects of modernity, particularly secularism and cultural pluralism. The term "Islamist" can include both devout Muslims who have little interest in politics and who evangelize on street corners by distributing Qurans, and political Muslims who would like to see the creation of an Islamic state or who in some way refer to Islamic principles in calling for social and political reforms that will create a more just, moral, and Islamic society. Political Islamists can include both moderates who work within the political system and seek to gain political power through elections and the more radical militants. The term "political Islamists" can also describe those who focus their energies more on creating a better society than on taking over the state and who have built schools, clinics, and cooperatives.

In recent years Islamism's appeal as a political movement has grown. However, political Muslims in many countries face a virtual police state that undermines or prohibits any attempt to build a mass-based political party or movement. In some Central Asian countries, anti-fundamentalism becomes the justification for severe abuses of human rights, and any person who is even moderately religious is labeled a fundamentalist and persecuted accordingly. Islamists face other obstacles to success. Many Muslims are wary of having their religion used for political purposes and do not have confidence in extreme Islamist movements.

Nonetheless, Islamists at the moment of this writing continue to gain popularity in many countries because they have established credibility in their communities, where they are seen as an alternative to corrupt, despotic governments in the pocket of the United States. Fawaz Gerges, professor of international affairs and Middle Eastern studies at Sarah Lawrence College and author of *America and Political Islam*, observes that if democratic elections were held, in almost every single country in the Muslim world Islamists would probably gain a majority. "They would obtain a majority because they are highly organized, they have established an effective social base, and they are seen to be quite legitimate by a sizeable number of Muslims" (*NCR*, Oct. 8, 2004).

For now, however, most countries in the Muslim world continue to exclude even moderate Islamists from power. Authoritarian secular regimes maintain their grip on the levers of government, and it remains to be seen whether they will yield to forces within their societies pressing for more popular participation.

ISLAMIC ACTIVISM

Two organizations have played a key role in the development of Islamic activism and Islamism. The Muslim Brotherhood, established in Egypt in 1928 by Hasan al-Banna, has had a tremendous influence on the Muslim world. Throughout its history the Muslim Brotherhood has stressed that Islam is not just a religion but a call to social action on behalf of the poor and downtrodden. To that end, the Muslim Brotherhood has established schools and clinics, instructed Muslims in labor law so that they could defend themselves from industrial exploitation, founded a modern scouting movement, opened factories where Muslims received better pay and benefits than they could obtain in the state sector, and taught prayer and Quranic living.

In its emphasis on social justice, the Muslim Brotherhood has been compared to Christian liberation theologians in Latin American, who also blur the distinction between religion and politics. Such groups as Hamas in Palestine and Hezbollah in Lebanon are the offshoots of the Muslim Brotherhood. These groups have vigorously, and sometimes violently, protested foreign occupation but have also implemented extensive social welfare programs to help the poorest members of society, from whom they have recruited many of their members. The Muslim Brotherhood has been suppressed in many Muslim countries but continues to have a wide popular following. In Egypt, the country where it was first established, the Brotherhood has not been allowed to compete in elections but commands significant support.

Another reformist organization that has been influential is the Jamaat-i-Islami (the Party of Islam), founded in India in 1941 by Mawlana Abul Ala Mawdudi (1903–1979). Mawdudi was an Indian journalist who spoke out against the secularism of the modern nation-state and argued for a universal jihad against colonialism, a struggle he called not just a right but a duty. He likened the barbarism and ignorance of the West to *jahiliyyah*, the unenlightened conditions existing in Arabia before the time of Muhammad. Mawdudi thought that the pure message of the Quran was the only basis for exercising political power; only an Islamic state could correct the decline into which Islam had fallen. Toward that end, he founded the Jamaat-i-Islami as a political party. He admired the discipline of the Communist Party and modeled the internal structure of his party upon it. But Jamaat-i-Islami was not intended to overthrow the state but to Islamicize the men who led it. The organization has played an important role in Pakistan; sister organizations of the group have been established in Bangladesh, Afghanistan, and Kashmir.

Both the Muslim Brotherhood and the Jamaat-i-Islami stressed the comprehensiveness of Islam. Islam was not just a religion but a system embracing the totality of human beings' needs and aspirations. While not advocating democracy per se, they embraced the modernist view of consultation and community consensus as essential to any government sanctioned by Islam. The Muslim Brotherhood and the Jamaat-i-Islami were attempts to modernize Islam by applying it to contemporary reality. Both advocated an Islamic alternative to the traditionalist ulama on the one hand and to Westernized elites on the other.

A thinker who preached social justice and has had enormous influence on radical Islam is the Egyptian revivalist Sayyid Qutb

(1906–1966). Qutb wrote that one could not expect hungry people to turn their thoughts to spiritual matters and that Islam must therefore direct itself to satisfying both people's material and spiritual needs. The eradication of poverty, therefore, became a major goal. Qutb felt that modern civilization had rebelled against the laws of God; it was necessary to reawaken high ideals, to acquaint humanity with a way of life that was harmonious with nature, positive, constructive, and still practicable. Qutb, who had briefly lived in the United States, saw the West as mired in decadence and thought that only Islam could provide a spiritual way forward.

Imprisoned for belonging to the Muslim Brotherhood by Egyptian president Gamal Abdel Nasser, who wanted to marginalize the role of religion in Egypt, Qutb concluded while in prison that secularists and religious Muslims could not live in peace in the same society. Whereas Mawdudi had compared the West to jahiliyyah, Qutb controversially likened contemporary Muslim societies to jahiliyyah. A man like Nasser was outwardly a Muslim but really an apostate to his religion and deserved to be overthrown.

Executed by the Egyptian government in 1966, Qutb was an opponent of nationalism, which he thought un-Islamic and counter to Muhammad's emphasis on the umma, the community of Muslim believers. Qutb's assertion that Muslims are answerable only to God, not to a sovereign state, became a key tenet for some contemporary Islamists, who assert that only an Islamic state that derives its laws from revelation has legitimacy.

Contemporary Islamists who are heirs to Qutb's philosophy also reject nationalism and try to reconcile Sunni and Shi'i differences. They consider the West too individualistic, favoring the rights of the individual over the rights of society and producing citizens who are buyers and consumers rather than creatures of God who find their fulfillment in living out God's will.

However, many Islamists are less focused on Islam as a spiritual answer to the dilemmas of mankind than as a practical solution to Muslims' social, economic, and political needs and to the problems of underemployment and corruption that plague many Muslim countries. Those most active in Islamist politics are often not particularly religious but are inspired by the belief that Islam as an ideology can address the needs of the state and society. Their hope is that political Islam can provide Muslim societies with a way forward where philosophies borrowed from the West have failed.

Islam as an ideology, not just a religion, has been put into practice in diverse ways. Those excluded from power have used Islam to clamor for reform and a greater voice in their society. States that have adopted Islam as a source of legitimacy have implemented very different regimes, from Saudi Arabia's conservative monarchy to Pakistan's military regime, to Iran's rule by a supremely guided jurist, to Libya's socialist state, where President Muammar Qaddafi has used Islam to support his unorthodox vision of an Arab populist alternative to capitalism and Marxism.

In all of these places, Islam as the guiding philosophy of the state has been given different interpretations. Perceptions of a monolithic Islamic threat ignore the complex reality of Islam; any discussion of Islam in general must give rise to the question of which Islam and whose Islam is being invoked.

ISLAM AND TERRORISM

The association of Islam with Islamism, and Islamism with terrorism, has been firmly fixed in the public mind by the Western media, which sometimes presents the face of Islamic fundamentalism as the face of Islam itself. Most Muslims are not fundamentalists, however, and most fundamentalists are not terrorists. But there are, undeniably, terrorists who are Muslims and who draw on—some say pervert—the tradition of the lesser jihad (defensive war) as well as on nineteenth-century European revolutionary anarchism.

Many of the extremists associated with Osama bin Laden participated in the international jihad against the Soviet Union in Afghanistan, where they received military training and indoctrination. After the war was over, these uprooted individuals did not integrate back into their respective societies but formed a clandestine transnational network unrestrained by the rule of law. They share a hatred for contemporary Muslim governments, often derived from time spent in jails where they were radicalized, and a deep distrust of popular organizations and action (Mamdani, *Good Muslim, Bad Muslim*, p. 170).

According to one writer, the Sunni Islamist groups that engage in jihad are all children of a constellation of influences that include the Muslim Brotherhood, Jamaat-i-Islami, and Wahhabism (Ali, *The Clash of Fundamentalism*, p. 177). Others have traced Muslim terrorism to the unfinished business of the Cold War, arguing that proxy wars funded by the United States in Afghanistan, Africa, and Latin America during the 1980s eroded the rule of law and provided training in terrorist methods that were then exported to other parts of the globe.

The French scholar Olivier Roy charges that the campaign of global jihadists (he calls them "neofundamentalists") involves a willed reconfiguration of what it means to be Muslim. The global jihadists transform the jihadist imperative from a collective responsibility of Muslims to defend their societies from aggression to an individual duty binding on each Muslim. This is an innovation and a departure from traditional Islam.

Roy describes the jihadists as Islamicizing the anti-imperialist resentment prompted by rich nations' dominance of technology and markets. Just as anti-globalization activists in Western countries have garnered some sympathy for their efforts, bin Laden and his followers attempt to create a wider sympathy for their cause by spectacular terror attacks. Such attacks are intended to mobilize other Muslims to join their struggle against corrupt "apostate" Muslim governments. For instance, Osama bin Laden has clearly stated his opposition to the Saudi ruling family and his desire to overthrow it. Opposition to the stationing of United States troops in Saudi Arabia and to United States policies in Iraq during the 1990s fueled bin Laden's 1996 declaration of jihad against the United States. He has also cited Israel's 1982 invasion of Lebanon and United States support for it as factors.

Roy describes the neo-fundamentalists as more a product of globalization than of an Islamic past. Many are Western-educated and middle- or upper-middle class and combine jihad against the West with a conservative view of Islam drawn more from Saudi Wahhabism than either traditional Islam or the revolutionary Islam of Iran. They perceive Western powers as mounting a Judeo-Christian conspiracy to destroy Muslim societies. Because they claim to be guided by religious imperatives, they contend that Muslims who do not rush to support them are wayward Muslims who cannot be considered proper Muslims at all and are even enemies of Islam.

However, Islamic terrorists are difficult to describe en masse because they may have many different agendas. Terrorists in Egypt who attacked tourists during the 1990s seemed to have hoped to paralyze the tourist trade and with it the political fortunes of Egyptian President Hosni Mubarak. The same appears true of more recent terrorist attacks in Egypt in 2006. Attacks launched by Hezbollah in Lebanon during the 1980s and 1990s focused on expelling foreign powers, whether France, Israel, or the United States, from the country. Foreign jihadists joining the insurgency in Iraq after the U.S. invasion have their own set of motivations, many of them linked to the Sunni/Shi'i rivalry for power. While pan-Islamists claim to transcend nationalism in their concern for the worldwide umma, the saying that all politics is local seems to describe Islamic terrorists as much as other people. The rhetoric of Islam often accompanies actions that are focused on much more specific concerns rooted in a particular nation or area.

In the wake of the terrorist attacks on September 11, 2001, Americans tend to see themselves and other Westerners as the primary targets of Muslim extremists, but a great many of the victims of Al-Qaeda have not been Westerners but other Muslims. Not surprisingly, many Muslims have generally responded with anger to the violent attacks waged by Al-Qaeda and groups affiliated with it and have been quick to repudiate any connections between Al-Qaeda-inspired violence and Islam. They point

out that Islam, like Christianity, has rules of warfare that pro-
hibit attacks on civilians and that bin Laden and his followers
are misusing Islam for their own purposes.

Unfortunately, while it is no fairer to judge Islam by the actions of bin Laden than to judge Christianity by the actions of
the Ku Klux Klan who burned crosses on the lawns of black
Americans, many still will be tempted to draw those inferences.
The actions of a small and violent minority have defined the face
of Islam for many Americans, even though the so-called "Islamic"
terrorists are driven by political, not religious, motives. That the
jihadists seek justification of their actions in the Quran says less
about their religious principles than about the continuing ability
of Islam to command Muslims' loyalty.

UNITED STATES POLICY

The United States government has pursued an inconsistent
policy with regard to Islam and Islamists. At times the United
States viewed Islam as an ally in its Cold War battle against communism and the Soviet Union—hence the American-funded
jihad against the Soviet Union, in which the United States fun-
neled money to the Afghan mujahideen fighting the Soviets, and,
indeed, to the most extremist Islamic groups among them rather
than toward more moderate factions. More often the United States
has shown a deep distrust of both nationalists and Islamists, fear-
ing that nationalism and/or Islamism will disturb the stable flow
of Middle East oil and spread revolution.

The Iranian revolution of 1979 and the seizure of United States
hostages who were kept for more than a year was a searing event for
the United States, creating images of Muslim radicals that still lin-
ger today in the American consciousness. Since then the United
States has tended to look at any Islamist movement through the
perspective of the Iranian revolution. Even though Iran has not
successfully exported its brand of revolutionary Islam to other
countries, the United States continues to be skeptical and indeed
hostile to movements that blend Islam with political goals. Such

religious-political movements challenge American beliefs about how modern countries should develop as well as secular presuppositions derived from the Enlightenment that regard religion as a belief system best confined to personal life.

The notable exception to this stance has been United States support for the Jewish religious-political movement known as Zionism. But whether because of the strategic importance of the Muslim Middle East or because of historic prejudices against Islam, Americans routinely stereotype movements inspired by Islam as fanatical. The worldwide Muslim resurgence is thus a challenge to United States policymakers to move beyond their own preconceptions to engage creatively with the multiple forms that political Islam is taking and to distinguish dangerous extremists from those whose point of view should be brought into the political process.

Muslim renewal challenges not only longstanding American policies that date back to World War II and the emergence of the United States as a superpower but also fundamental American principles and values. Both the United States and its allies among the authoritarian regimes that dominate the Muslim world view democracy as a potential threat, one that raises the possibility of client states metamorphosing into more independent nations that might make Western access to oil more expensive and/or less reliable. Yet United States support for oppressive, nondemocratic regimes fuels Muslim radicalism and betrays core American values. Because of this, President George W. Bush recently announced a new United States commitment to supporting democracy in the Middle East. Whether this commitment is borne out in deeds as well as words remains to be seen.

THE CLASH OF CULTURES AND CIVILIZATIONS

Today there is much talk about the clash of cultures. In popular newspapers and magazines, Islam and the West are sometimes portrayed as inextricably locked in conflict, and enduring and usually unflattering attributes are ascribed to either side. In the West, Muslims are portrayed as ignorant, fanatical, violent, and primitive. Equally unflattering depictions of Americans circulate in the mass media read by Muslims, where Americans are presented as greedy, exploitative, decadent, and bent on destroying Islam.

With interfaith and intercultural relations strained, Christians, Muslims, and Jews are challenged to go beyond the stereotypes and to reach a greater understanding of each other's religious beliefs and the geopolitical situation of Muslims, Christians, and Jews in the world today. The keen sense of humiliation that some Muslims feel about the relegation of a once-great Islamic civilization to numerous semi-dependent Western fiefdoms and the bitterness among some Jews about Christian anti-Semitism may put a special burden on Christians, particularly American Christians. The United States is the sole superpower in the world today. Because of the power it commands, the United States makes decisions that influence people's lives the world over. Preoccupied with their own personal lives, Americans are often unaware of what these decisions are and how they affect other countries and peoples. Oblivious to what their government does in their name, they are surprised and even disbelieving when United States policies create resentment or hostility.

Citizenship brings with it responsibility. Wealth, power, and privilege only add to this. American Christians today are challenged to understand the situation of those living in other parts of the world. Doing so requires attention to history—the troubled history of Christian-Muslim interaction as well as the history of Western colonization of Muslim lands. The tensions that currently exist between Muslims and the West are driven more by geopolitical issues that go ignored in the mass media than by religion. Americans would do well to consider the international competition for resources, the human rights record of foreign governments and their own, the economic role the United States plays in Muslim countries, and United States support for authoritarian regimes in the Muslim world, for these are the issues that most inflame relations between the United States and Muslims. Though people talk about a clash of cultures between the West and Muslims, Muslims are also a product of the West, and the much-referred-to clash of cultures often conceals a clash of economic and political interests.

Religious ignorance and bigotry enable both Western and Muslim leaders to appeal to popular prejudice for support instead of talking about specific current issues that have fostered hostility. It is interesting to bear in mind the late Professor Edward Said's observation in his book, *Covering Islam: How the Media and the Experts Determine How We See the Rest of the World*, that the topic of Islam only began to surface in the Western media as a problem to be addressed following the rise in oil prices in 1973. Said, a Palestinian Christian and professor at Columbia University, contends that a colonialist perspective governs coverage of Islam, held by people who are unconscious of the history of colonialism.

It may be that the fear and hostility with which Muslims and Americans currently regard each other can refocus attention on religion in a positive way. Americans who are serious about their religious faith may be better able to understand and sympathize with Muslims' desire to live in a more faith-centered world than their secularist fellow-Americans. Religious believers of all faiths see God as the cornerstone of the world, and the insistence of many Muslims that sovereignty rests with God, not imperfect human beings, will strike them as true rather than irrational or dogmatic.

Certainly, Muslims and American Christians can only benefit from learning more about each other's religion. The message of both Christianity and Islam is peace. As much as religion has been often misused to fuel political animosities, it is by returning to the message of Christ and the prophet Muhammad that we can find inspiration to live with each other compassionately, justly, and peacefully.

Bibliography

Abootalebi, Ali R. "Islam, Islamists, and Democracy," *Middle East Review of International Affairs*, Vol. 3, No. 1 (March 1999). http://www.biu.ac.il/SOC/besa/meria/journal/1999/issues1,jv3n1a2.html.

Abou El Fadl, Khaled. "Commentary: Terrorism Is at Odds with Islamic Tradition," Muslim Lawyers Guild, http://www.muslimlawyers.net/news/index.php3?aktion=show&number=78.

_____. "Islam and the Theology of Power," *Middle East Report*, http://www.merip.org/mer/mer221/221_abu_el_fadl.html.

Ahmed, Akbar S. *Islam Today: A Short Introduction to the Muslim World*. London; New York: I. B. Tauris, 2002, ©1999.

Ali, Tariq. *The Clash of Fundamentalisms: Crusades, Jihads and Modernity*. London: Verso, 2003.

Armstrong, Karen. *Islam: A Short History*. New York: Random House, 2000.

_____. *The Battle for God: A History of Fundamentalism*. New York: Ballantine Books, 2001.

Aslan, Reza. *No god but God: The Origins, Evolution, and Future of Isalm*. New York: Random House, 2006.

Baker, William W. *More in Common than You Think: The Bridge Between Islam and Christianity*. Las Vegas, NV: Defenders Publications, 1998.

Çapan, Ergün, ed. *An Islamic Perspective: Terror and Suicide Attacks*. Somerset, NJ: The Light, Inc. 2004.

Dardess, George. *Meeting Islam: A Guide for Christians*. Brewster, MA: Paraclete Press, 2005.

Denny, Frederick Matthewson. *An Introduction to Islam*. 2nd ed. New York: Macmillan Publishing Company, 1994.

Elias, Jamal J., adapted by Nancy D. Lewis. *The Pocket Idiot's Guide to Islam*. London: Laurence King Publishing Ltd., 2002.

Ellis, Kail C. *The Vatican, Islam, and the Middle East*. Syracuse, NY: Syracuse University Press, 1987.

Ernst, Carl. W. *Following Muhammad: Rethinking Islam in the Contemporary World*. Chapel Hill: University of North Carolina Press, 2003.

Esposito, John L. *Islam: The Straight Path*. New York: Oxford University Press, 1991.

_____. *The Islamic Threat: Myth or Reality?* 3rd ed. New York: Oxford University Press, 1999.

_____. *What Everyone Needs to Know about Islam*. New York: Oxford University Press, 2002.

Gerges, Fawaz A. *America and Political Islam: Clash of Cultures or Clash of Interests*. Cambridge, NY: Cambridge University Press, 1999.

Gorenberg, Gershom. *The End of Days: Fundamentalism and the Struggle for the Temple Mount*. New York: Free Press, 2000.

Hodgson, Marshall G. S. *The Venture of Islam*. Chicago: University of Chicago Press, 1974.

Hurley, Jennifer A., ed. *Islam: Opposing Viewpoints*. San Diego: Greenhaven Press, 2001.

Jomier, Jacques. *How to Understand Islam*. New York: Crossroad Publishing, 1989.

Lawrence, Bruce B. *Shattering the Myth: Islam beyond Violence*. Princeton, NJ: Princeton University Press, 1998.

Lippman, Thomas W. *Understanding Islam: An Introduction to the Muslim World*. New York: Penguin, 1995.

Lowney, Chris. *A Vanished World: Medieval Spain's Golden Age of Enlightenment*. New York: Free Press, 2005.

Mamdani, Mahmood. *Good Muslim, Bad Muslim: America, the Cold War and the Roots of Terror*. New York: Three Leaves Press, Doubleday, 2005.

Martin, Richard C. *Islamic Studies: A History of Religions Approach*. 2nd ed. Englewood Cliffs, NJ: Prentice-Hall, 1982.

Nasr, Seyyed Hossein. *The Heart of Islam: Enduring Values for Humanity*. San Francisco: HarperSan Francisco, 2002.

_____. *Islam: Religion, History, and Civilization*. San Francisco: Harper San Francisco, 2003.

Patterson, Margot. "Islamic Fundamentalism Feared, Misunderstood," *National Catholic Reporter*, Oct. 8, 2004.

Peters, F. E. *Islam: A Guide for Jews and Christians*. Princeton, NJ: Princeton University Press, 2003.

Rodenbeck, Max. "The Truth about Jihad," Review of *Osama: The Making of a Terrorist* by Jonathan Randal, *Globalized Islam: The Search for a New Ummah* by Olivier Roy, and *The War for Muslim Minds: Islam and the West* by Gilles Kepel, translated from the French by Pascale Ghazalah, *The New York Review of Books*, Aug. 11, 2005.

Sageman, Marc. "Understanding Terror Networks," Foreign Policy Research Institute, Nov. 1, 2004, http://www.fpri.org/enbdones/ 20041101.middleast.sageman.understandingterrornetworks .html.

Said, Edward W. *Covering Islam: How the Media and the Experts Determine How We See the Rest of the World*. New York: Vintage Books, ©1981, 1997.

Speight, R. Marston. *God Is One: The Way of Islam*. New York: Friendship Press, ©1989.

Urban II (1095), *Speech at the Council of Clermont, 1095*. Retrieved June 25, 2006, from http://www.fordham.edu/halsall/source/urban 2-5vers.html.

Index